Palgrave Pivots in Sports Economics

Series Editors
Wladimir Andreff
Emeritus Professor
University Paris 1 Panthéon-Sorbonne
Paris, France

Andrew Zimbalist
Department of Economics
Smith College
Northampton, MA, USA

This mid-length monograph series invites contributions between 25,000–50,000 words in length, and considers the economic analysis of sports from all aspects, including but not limited to: the demand for sports, broadcasting and media, sport and health, mega-events, sports accounting, finance, betting and gambling, sponsorship, regional development, governance, competitive balance, revenue sharing, player unions, pricing and ticketing, regulation and anti-trust, and, globalization. Sports Economics is a rapidly growing field and this series provides an exciting new publication outlet enabling authors to generate reach and impact.

John Embery

Attendance Demand in Sports Economics

A New Methodological Approach

John Embery
Leeds Business School
Leeds Beckett University
Leeds, UK

ISSN 2662-6438   ISSN 2662-6446   (electronic)
Palgrave Pivots in Sports Economics
ISBN 978-3-031-60039-5   ISBN 978-3-031-60040-1   (eBook)
https://doi.org/10.1007/978-3-031-60040-1

This Palgrave Macmillan imprint is published by the registered company Springer Nature Switzerland AG.
The registered company address is: Gewerbestrasse 11, 6330 Cham, Switzerland

Paper in this product is recyclable.

CONTENTS

LIST OF TABLES

CHAPTER 1

Introduction

Abstract In this brief introduction to this short book, I provide concise summaries of the three main chapters which constitute its main content. The chapter breakdowns are based on the abstracts for the three main chapters; in these I highlight the thematic structure. There is a debate to be had that is not currently being had regarding economic theory of sports attendance demand. That debate turns on a contrast between the standard economic agent and the social nature of attendance demand. A different approach to attendance demand is possible.

Keywords Attendance demand • Methodology • Economic agent • Critical realism

The three main chapters that constitute this short book follow a simple theme. Theory, method and research in sports economics focused on attendance demand takes its concept of an 'agent' (the decisionmaker) from the discipline at large. This agent makes decisions based on given preferences and with reference to a 'budget constraint'. The starting point, however, is isolated self-interested decision-making. This is a form of 'atomism' and is quite different than starting from an agent who has been

© The Author(s), under exclusive license to Springer Nature Switzerland AG 2024
J. Embery, *Attendance Demand in Sports Economics*, Palgrave Pivots in Sports Economics,
https://doi.org/10.1007/978-3-031-60040-1_1

socialised and encultured as a supporter or fan. As a long-suffering Preston North End FC football fan who has over 25 years taught courses on microeconomics, behavioural economics and sports economics, this has always struck me as odd.

I first started to think about how to articulate my concerns and explore the degree to which they are warranted in 2003 when first writing a degree module on sports economics. There were relatively few undergraduate textbooks on the subject and dedicated academic journals had only started to appear at the end of the 1990s. Over the years teaching from this material reinforced my sense that there was an obvious mismatch that warranted investigation. When I finally got round to writing about the subject, I realised the problem naturally decomposed into three simple parts.

In Chap. 1 I undertake a detailed survey of published sports economics articles dealing with attendance demand. This is not a simple 'state of the field review'. It is rather a critical review of the conceptualisation of the agent. This work confirmed my impression that the agent is appropriated from the field at large (what we might call 'the mainstream') and is adapted to sports economics, especially in work undertaken since the advent of dedicated journals. I identify the limits this places on developments in the field, including the limited use made of the potential of behavioural economics, and make the simple point that there is a debate to be had, which is not currently being had regarding the appropriateness of this agent.

In Chap. 2 I develop an argument focused on the terms of debate. The core of the chapter contrasts a participant observation ethnographic account of 'a day at the football' with the standard economic agent used or presupposed in theory and research on attendance demand. This leads to the question, 'is it reasonable to think that the person who attended a sports event of the kind described becomes some version of the standard economic agent at the point of purchase of the ticket that secures attendance?' The contrast leads to a discussion of the difference this makes and this in turn leads to reflection on why it is that the standard economic agent is used. I place this in the context of a broader 'divide' in economics and suggest that sports economics finds itself on one side of this divide. I then briefly discuss possible conceptual resources that might place attendance demand on the other side of the divide but also suggest a fuller account remains to be provided.

In Chap. 3 I set out an alternative approach to theory and research in attendance demand, which places the agent on the other side of the divide I have previously identified. I begin from the question, 'if we don't start from the standard economic agent, what does a theory of and research strategy for sports attendance demand look like?' I make the case that it makes sense to 'go back to basics' in order to place attendance demand on the other side of the divide. To do this I draw on critical realism and combine this with behavioural economics. I then provide a 'sketch' of a research strategy that brings these together.

To summarise the thematic structure is:

1. There is a debate to be had.
2. That debate turns on a contrast between the standard economic agent and the social nature of attendance demand.
3. A different approach to attendance demand is possible, which situates the agent quite differently.

Clearly, the main focus of this short book is methodological. Its originality lies in the overview it provides of the field and the insight it offers regarding a fundamental issue. It requires considerable experience and long years of reading to be in a position to write a book like this. Moreover, it should also be clear that the intended wider audience is one that has not been encouraged to engage with methodology (and in my case ontology). This required careful thought regarding a writing strategy, which might be summarised as simple but not simplistic, engaging but not overly partisan.

CHAPTER 2

The Curious Case of the Missing Social Agent in Sports Economics

Abstract In this chapter I explore an extensive survey of published literature on the economics of sports attendance demand. I break this down into publication before and after the establishment of dedicated sports economics journals. My focus is the concept of an economic agent and I make the case that this has, for various reasons, been adopted and adapted from the discipline at large. I argue that this has definite limits since sports attendance is a quintessentially social activity and this sits awkwardly with this concept of an agent. This leads to the conclusion that there is a debate to be had which has not yet been had.

Keywords Sports economics • Attendance demand • Decision-making • Economic agent

Bobby Robson, the archetypical Football Man, once asked 'What is a club in any case?' and then nailed the definition of it in eighty-one words, imagining his beloved Newcastle as he did so. 'Not the buildings or the directors or the people who are paid to represent it,' said Robson. 'It's not the television contracts, get-out clauses, marketing departments or executive boxes. It's the noise, the passion, the feelings of belonging, the pride in your city. It's a small boy clambering up the stadium steps for the first time, gripping his

J. Embery, *Attendance Demand in Sports Economics*, Palgrave Pivots in Sports Economics,
https://doi.org/10.1007/978-3-031-60040-1_2

father's hand, gasping at the hallowed stretch of turf beneath him and, without being able to do a thing about it, falling in love.
Hamilton, D. (2018) *Going to the Match*, pp. 21–22

INTRODUCTION

Who sits at the centre of the model of demand for attendance at professional sport events?[1] The obvious answer is an economic agent. The agent in research on the demand for sport is either explicitly appropriated from the 'mainstream'—a standard repository of state of the art for the economics profession—or implicitly invokes that agent.[2] This is odd. Mainstream microeconomics describes the agent as a highly focused rational calculative entity, who prefers more to less and most to least. The agent is constructed from axioms, typically endowed with unlimited cognitive resources and is assumed to be the relevant decisionmaker in all situations that have a transactional component.[3] They are in this sense universal, but most importantly, the decisions they make are individual—they are self-regarding and taken in isolation from others. Various methodologists and philosophers of economics have referred over the years to the approach as methodological individualism and to the isolation as 'atomism' (for range of philosophers interested in the subject see, e.g. Blaug, 1992; Mäki,

[1] Note: throughout the chapter I switch between use of 'I' and 'we' as appropriate to context. Throughout the chapter I mainly refer to attendance demand, but the issues apply more generally to demand for spectation which may or may not be in person and different scholars who I draw on for the literature use a variety of terms.

[2] Note: there is an extensive literature which discusses the many uses of the term 'neoclassical' economics and which distinguishes mainstream economics and a concept of orthodox economics. For use of terminology see Dequech (2007). For a popular summary of core commitments of 'neoclassical' economics, see Arnsperger and Varoufakis (2006). For debate concerning the many meanings, see Morgan (2016a, 2016b).

[3] Note: I will be discussing the difference behavioural economics makes to this statement regarding cognitive resources in later work.

2001; Lawson, 1997, 2003).[4] Demand for sport is quintessentially a social decision. It is the very antithesis of atomistic.

In this chapter I argue that the appropriation of a mainstream economic agent requires explanation and warrants reconsideration. This chapter is not a state of the field review. Nor is it a chapter on organisational aspects of demand for attendance at sports events. These topics have been covered sufficiently in earlier work (see Schofield, 1983, Cairns et al., 1986, Borland & MacDonald, 2003, Villar & Guerrero, 2009, Schreyer & Ansari, 2022, for extensive reviews of demand for sport across the last four decades). This chapter is rather a critical review of the conceptualisation of the agent at the centre of sports economics. It thus explores key survey articles and other sources of literature, but in the form of a constructive 'immanent critique'.

To be clear, reflection on the adequacy of the concept of human agency has received relatively little critical coverage in sports economics literature. The majority of work on demand for sport focuses on the organisational aspects; they pay little or no attention to the nature of the decisionmaker and how they are represented, despite the centrality of demand concepts in the sports economics research literature (Schreyer & Ansari, 2022). In this chapter I focus on the way sports economists have neglected the heterogeneity of agents and crucially the *sociality* of the agent in the consumption of sport—the embeddedness of the agent in social relations.[5] Social aspects of spectating sports have existed as an integral part of culture for millennia. Mainstream economics usually assumes away most of the social context which determines how things happen and what people do. This is deemed part of other disciplines such as sociology, anthropol-

---

[4] See also Cartwright (2007); Davis (2003); Fullbrook (2002a, 2002b).; Hodgson (2004, 2007). Note: the concept of an economic agent is no single person's invention. It is the product of years of development mainly in microeconomics. Theory and models always have a decisionmaker. This can be the firm, the consumer, the investor, the employee and so on. Often their range of choices, that is what they can do and do; in fact, do is a product of a mathematical construct. Histories of economics trace this back to the marginal revolution—Stanley Jevons, Alfred Marshall and so on—albeit Marshall was conflicted about the role of mathematics. In the twentieth century the increasing formalisation of economic theory placed the utility function and then revealed preference at the heart of microeconomics. The agent (representative or otherwise) has been basic to formal theory of market activity and market structure and so on. For early references see, for example, Samuelson (1937, 1938a, 1938b, 1938c, 1938d). More recent versions tend to be built around the Savage axioms on Bayesian updating (Karni, 2016; the main focus is expected utility theory [Machina, 2008]).

[5] The definition of sociality is important here. Mason and Shan (2017, p. 3) define sociality as 'any significant deviation from behaviour exhibited by an individual when that individual is within a group of two or more'.

ogy, psychology or politics, albeit mainstream economics does now have sub-disciplines that seek to draw to some degree on these, such as behavioural economics. I argue, however, that insofar as sports economics has appropriated or implicitly presupposed the standard mainstream economic agent, there is a basic blind spot in the understanding of demand for sport. While we still tend to think of 'the economy' as a combination of production and finance, sports and culture are now significant parts of that economy[6] and sports economics must embrace the wider social sciences if it is to remain relevant.[7]

As we shall establish, the mainstream model of the utility maximising, rational, income-constrained *atomised* consumer has been the dominant approach in the economic analysis of sport from the early 1970s until the present day. The conceptualisation of demand for sport attendance has been a subset of this. In the twenty-first century there has been some sign of diversity; however, this has had sharp limits. Published research has become less formalistic, and in some cases interdisciplinary, but the central conceptualisation remains the standard economic agent. There are various reasons for this.

The long-established axioms and assumptions of microeconomic theory are deeply embedded and therefore the contemporary research literature has obvious reasons to draw upon it, since otherwise one faces the criticism that one is 'not doing economics'. This is especially so early on in the development of the field or sub-discipline when one is likely to be publishing in journals not devoted to sports economics. If one wishes to be taken seriously within the discipline, one draws on its standard concepts, and these are, in any case, assumed to be universal. Sports economics is in this sense in no different a position than any other sub-disciplinary focus. As such, its practitioners may feel no need to define or justify use of the concept of an agent and any reconceptualisation does not stray far from the basic characteristics of the mainstream agent and always take it as a point of reference. Often it simply serves as a point of departure or as a background that can be briefly referred to or used as a well-understood language form ('we all know what we mean'). This remains the case as the

---

[6] For example, attendance records show that approximately 226 million people attended the 18 most popular sports leagues in 2021 (Statista, 2022a). Revenues for the year were estimated at $21 billion (Statista, 2022b). Attendance at stadia has grown throughout the last century and a half.

[7] Bryson et al. (2015) state four reasons why sport and the study of sport economics are relevant and must remain so. The first two are to be expected in economic study: it is big business, and it is a significant employer. The third reason is that it is a core experience and source of meaning to ordinary people—in standard terminology consumption of sport is a source of 'satisfaction'. The fourth is that sports economics sheds light on fundamental economic questions.

field or sub-discipline develops and acquires its own journals and is surely reinforced insofar as there has been little or no discussion of what a decision-making economic 'agent' might actually 'look like' in the context of demand for commercial sports. Yet, given a moment's reflection, the continued influence of the mainstream concept of agency must surely strike non-economists as odd. Demand for attendance at sports events is so obviously a heterogeneous *social* activity. Nobody would go to watch Preston North End Football club play on a cold, wet, November evening if decision-making were merely an individual rational act of optimisation (and no resort to 'given preferences' can credibly lead one to think otherwise).

I explore the issues in four sections. In Sect. 'Early Papers in Sports Economics' I set the scene. I begin from the earliest papers on sports economics, published in the 1950s to the early 1970s. These papers became early reference sources for the works in demand for sport published thereafter. These papers were published in general economics journals. In Sect. '"State of the Field" Review Papers' I move on to explore 'State of the Field' review papers and in Sect. 'The Advent of Dedicated Sports Economics Journals' I turn to publication in new, dedicated sports management and economics journals. This began around the turn of the millennium with the publication of the *Sports Management Review* in 1998 and *Journal of Sports Economics* in 2000 but gained momentum from 2008. In Sect. 'The Breakout Period from 2008' titled the 'break out period from 2008' I draw on my own analysis of papers on sports attendance published in *Journal of Sports Economics*, and in 'the changed scene', I highlight the degree to which the field has diversified and the constraints that can be observed. Sections 'Early Papers in Sports Economics' and '"State of the Field" Review Papers' speak to the same underlying issue: there has been little focus on the adequacy of the concept of a decision-making agent in the study of demand for sports. Section 'The Advent of Dedicated Sports Economics Journals' and what follows highlight both the development and constraints of the field. I conclude with brief discussion of possible sources one might draw on in developing a more 'social agent' appropriate to attendance demand in sports economics.

EARLY PAPERS IN SPORTS ECONOMICS

Today, attendance demand is widely written about in sports economics. The first papers worthy of comment, however, did not start with a main focus on attendance demand and the agent. The earliest foray into sports economics is widely cited as Rottenberg's 1956 paper on the baseball labour market. The paper's central thrust is that it is the institutional arrangements of labour markets that are of primary concern. The concept of demand is merely incorporated as part of the discussion and invokes the standard mainstream agent. The next major paper commonly cited as highly influential is Neale (1964). While the title of this paper is provocative in the context of the issues we raised in the introduction, 'The Peculiar Economics of Professional Sports', the peculiarity referred to is not the nature of agency in sports demand but rather that the economics of sport appears to run counter to the expected competitive markets in theory of the firm. So, according to Neale the firm, 'vis-à-vis our accepted way of looking at the firm in a competitive market ... is not the firm as understood in economic theory' (Neale, 1964, p. 4). Neale describes the organisation of professional sports as similar to natural monopoly and observes:

> The firm of economic theory is the league, and the league is a natural monopoly with demand and cost and profit adjustments always tending toward unification of all league-firms into a single firma-firmorum. (Neale, 1964, p. 4)

Whilst not explicitly acknowledging the sociality of sporting events, the paper has a clear message. Sport and attendance at sports events does not fit neatly into the usual conceptualisation of competitive markets and of demand, and sports economists should recognise this. Hence, 'the firm of economic analysis; and the item sold by the sporting firm is not the product of these firms, or not entirely' (Neale, 1964, p. 2). Moreover, sport is marked by definite peculiarities in structure and function, dependent on collusion and interdependence with 'interrelated streams of utility' (Neale, 1964, p. 3).

One might think these initial concerns would lead to future research that focused on what made sports economics in general and sports attendance in particular different. However, despite that the paper attracted attention, Neale's methodological concerns were mainly overlooked. This is evident if we move on to Sloane (1971). This paper is widely recognised today as seminal. The title of Sloane's paper tells one everything you need to know here about the direction of travel the field was taking, 'The economics of professional football: the football club as utility maximiser'. To its credit, Sloane's contribution highlights the importance of institutional arrangements and thus the need to consider what is, in this sense, different regarding the economics of sport. However, Sloane explicitly introduces the mainstream concepts of utility and profit maximisation and does so without feeling it necessary to discuss why. Arguably, this laid the ground for the introduction of the whole conceptualisation of demand one finds in mainstream microeconomics from that time, and this, of course, includes the agent.

The earliest publication focused on sports attendance demand was Noll's aptly titled 'Attendance and price setting' (Noll, 1974). Its subject was the major American sports leagues. This paper became a significant touchstone, especially for US sports economists. The paper adopts a format that any mainstream economist would recognise. The paper takes a dataset and runs regressions for the 1970 and 1971 baseball seasons in order to derive findings regarding elasticity and the response to prices. The whole is constructed around a standard mainstream economic agent. Following Noll the mainstream conceptualisation of demand became, with few exceptions, the default for research on sports attendance.[8] This is so both in terms of explicit use of concepts and in terms of implicit frame of reference for how attendance is conceived (see Borland & MacDonald, 2003). This was to remain the case until the launch of a dedicated journal for sports economics in 2000, Journal of Sorts Economics, at which point some degree of diversity emerged, a point we will return to. In any case, Noll's paper was followed by a series of methodologically similar articles. One might describe these as estimating demand characteristics using a rational choice framework that depends on the standard economic agent.

It should be noted, however, that during the 1970s and into the 1980s academic research on sports economics was relatively scarce and as intimated above there was no dedicated sports economics journal. Very little was published in the main non-specialist economics journals, nor was there explicit editorial encouragement for papers on the subject. It is, therefore, unsurprising that economists wishing to publish on the subject would think carefully about what might be needed to publish in a non-specialist journal. 'Following the field' was arguably the rational response, given that the economic agent assumed in economics is a universal agent and it might be more difficult to be published if one took an entirely different point of view that might be deemed to repudiate this. The

---

[8] Note: there are exceptions, but these tend to be within other social science fields such as sociology. Importantly, these are not categorised as 'economics' research. Some are referred to as interdisciplinary. I briefly discuss the issues this raises later.

experience of others across many sub-disciplines of economics at the time speaks to this concern (see, e.g. the difficulty future Nobel laureate George Akerlof had in getting his 'The market for lemons' published).[9] Moreover, anyone educated in economics during the heyday of what has come to be known as 'formalism', when 'pure theory' dominated economics research and economics was undertaking an expansion into many new areas of research, would not have been encouraged by that education to think about this adoption of the standard mainstream economic agent.[10] Recall that in the mid-1980s the Chicago School Nobel laureate George Stigler was referring to economics as 'the imperial science', by which he meant it had been 'aggressive in addressing central problems in a considerable number of neighbouring social disciplines, and without any invitations' (Stigler, 1984, p. 311)—and if one wants a sense of the perceived success this achieved, one need only Google Stigler's Chicago School colleague Gary Becker.

'State of the Field' Review Papers

However, despite the relative scarcity of work published in sports economics in general and sports attendance in particular, sufficient research articles were eventually published to facilitate review essays. For the purpose of our argument Cairns et al.'s (1986) review essay, a survey of 'theory and evidence', is particularly interesting for what it indicates about what theoretical concepts were deemed of importance in the 1980s. It includes the statement:

> As was the case with objectives, the nature of the demand function is also of importance for virtually every aspect of club and league behaviour. Whatever objective function is assumed, club decisions on investment and pricing policies, and league choices over structure, scheduling and rules are all likely to be influenced strongly by demand considerations. Whether the purpose is to explain observed behaviour, to justify particular policies or to inform future decision-making, a detailed knowledge of the demand function is invaluable, for demand impinges on virtually all of the interesting questions in the area. (Cairns et al., 1986, p. 12)

---

[9] Visit: https://www.nobelprize.org/prizes/economic-sciences/2001/akerlof/article/.

[10] For a discussion of formalism see, for example, Blaug (2003); Boylan and O'Gorman (2007); and for historical context see Weintraub (2002).

This is instructive and reinforces what we have argued so far, but, we would suggest, is also indicative of what was to follow and that was almost two more decades of studies whose main focus was estimating demand characteristics using a rational choice framework with all that entails for the nature of the economic agent.

It is perhaps worth pausing here to introduce a few comments about the nature of the economic agent. Recall what I said about 'atomism' in the introduction. As we noted and as readers are no doubt also aware, the standard mainstream economic agent is constructed along methodological individualist lines and the method of estimating demand characteristics usually requires assumptions of isolation of variables. It typically looks to specify quantified relations and these are, if one thinks about it, of the fundamental form, 'whenever x occurs, y follows'. Critics refer to this as a 'constant conjunction' focused methodological approach (e.g. Lawson, 1997, 2015a, 2015b). It assumes that some aspect of reality can be represented or accounted for by a method of isolation which focuses on repetition of outcomes and restricts this to a few key variables or concepts. Everything else is excluded or somehow controlled for. Clearly, this is problematic if the subject matter is heterogeneous and based on complex social relationships (e.g. Hodgson, 2004; Davis, 2003, 2011). The approach seems to assume away much of what might be relevant to how things happen and why people do what they do. I would suggest this is exactly the problem sports economics has found itself coping with and its root source is the legacy the sub-discipline has inherited from the discipline at large.[11]

To reiterate, the field of sports economics has been encouraged to produce research that has aligned with pre-existing ways of doing things outside the field, irrespective of whether these were the most appropriate building blocks for theory and research in sports economics, and especially sports attendance. To be clear, the fundamental problem here may not be obvious to many in the field since there has been so little consideration of the nature of the agent. The concept has received little attention; it has either been presupposed in discussion or appropriated along with the broader frameworks of microeconomics. For example, Schofield's

[11] There is a great deal more to say here and a specific philosophical and methodological terminology to become familiar with, notably, 'ontology', methods based on 'deduction' and which presuppose 'closed systems'. See, for example, in economics, Dow (1997). For the philosophical background see, for example, Bhaskar (2008); Groff (2008, 2017).

'Performance and attendance at professional team sports', a review essay in Journal of Sports Behaviour (a sports journal but not a dedicated economics of sports journal), surveys 17 papers on aspects of demand for sports attendance, and none of these refer explicitly to the nature of the economic agent, but all frame their discussion or research in terms of the language of the standard mainstream microeconomic framework (Schofield, 1983).

If we return to Cairns et al.'s essay (1986), its demand analysis section surveys 11 papers, and these include the use of the concept of 'uncertainty of outcome'. The hypothesis of uncertainty of outcome relates to the perception that consumers value the inherent uncertainty of sports and that the organisational arrangements of sports competition should seek to maximise such uncertainty in order to maintain fan interest. This is very different than Keynes's well-known concept of fundamental uncertainty (or Frank Knights's version of the same). It is rather about how to match utility-maximising consumer behaviour to profit-maximising organisation. There is no discussion in the survey essay of the adequacy of the underlying concept of an agent, but there is discussion of the 'appropriate functional form of the demand equation' in relation to attendance demand. As such, there is no attempt to provide wider context or critical commentary on the nature of the agent. It is simply accepted as an integral part of existent theory.

One might argue that critique is not necessarily the purpose of a state of the field survey, but if we allow that sports attendance is a social act then it seems odd that the glaring mismatch does not at least invite some comment. What one does get, however, is comment on the nature and limits of research methods and while this is interesting it does follow a format that is quite familiar in economics. They note that the research may suffer from weak model specification and problems of data collection and rather pointedly state, 'fans were asked questions such as why they attended games in person and what determined the selection of games that they attended. Economists tend to shy away from such analyses; they prefer to observe behaviour rather than hear descriptions of how individuals claim to behave' (Cairns et al., 1986, p. 24). This is telling regarding the attitude to what constitutes legitimate empirical material and method. It is unfortunate though that the authors did not feel it necessary to pursue the implications for the nature of work done by economists. Fans own understanding of what they did and why were not a main concern for economists, but one might argue they are absolutely vital to any social understanding of an agent.

Moving on, the most widely cited review article on demand for sport not published in a dedicated sports economics journal was published in the prestigious Oxford Review of Economic Policy. Borland and MacDonald (2003) survey more than 60 research papers in this review, which under examination, either explicitly or implicitly, assume the agent we have discussed, and while previous published survey essays did not have much to say about the nature of the economic agent, Borland and MacDonald (2003) do. This may perhaps be because the intervening 15 years or so had provided time for the sub-discipline to embed and develop a sense of its own professional identity, albeit one bearing the imprint of mainstream microeconomics. The paper was published shortly after the establishment of the first dedicated sports economics journal, but as a retrospective it provides a useful snapshot of the previous period. In the section on theoretical perspective, the authors state that:

> the economic theory of demand for attendance at sporting events is based on a standard consumer-theory model. A representative consumer is assumed to choose a consumption bundle to maximise utility, subject to a budget constraint. (Borland & MacDonald, 2003, pp. 480–481)

The discussion of consumption bundles, consumed over a specified time-period, within a budget constraint, requiring choice and a resultant opportunity cost is built out of the now familiar economic agent. Moreover, Borland and MacDonald assert that based on the literature, consumer preferences in the case of demand for sport have similar properties to other goods and services. They do note, however, that utility in the essays surveyed is measured as an aggregated score of the quality of events attended. This is implicitly cumulative in a way that standard microeconomic treatments are not. It is an ex-post metric rather than the ex-ante assumption of standard rational choice theory. One could say this is economic theory adapting to the specific characteristics of the subject matter, but if it is the concession still takes the mainstream agent as its point of departure in order to develop modifications, one might question how significant the difference is.

It is still the case that in rational choice theory the choice decision that attendees make is prior to consumption and has utility at the point of decision as an incomplete estimation of expected utility. The assumption is that with full and complete information, the ex-ante utility yield is identical to the ex-post experience. However, since one cannot know how things will turn out or what feelings and experiences one will have or be subjected to based on (if we adopt language specific to some sports) organising getting to and from the match, events on the pitch, events off the pitch, one's own interactions at the match and the games eventual outcome, then there is an intrinsic uncertainty regarding the ex-post state and likely a frequent mismatch between ex-ante and any ex-post state for each match attended and this is also likely cumulative match by match as the season unfolds. Clearly, there is more to say about what this implies.

One might also note that the modification to theory does not address whether a simple concept of individual satisfaction adequately captures the motives and experiences of sports attendance. It is clear, moreover, that Borland and MacDonald are aware that this might be the case since they recognise that, similarity of properties of consumer preferences notwithstanding, 'there is a greater degree of complexity about preferences for attendance at a sporting contest than for most other goods and services' (Borland & MacDonald, 2003, p. 481) and they further acknowledge that habits, conspicuous consumption and bandwagon effects are present in such decisions. However, this is as far as it goes. There is no discussion of whether this might require a substantively different approach and no criticism along these lines of the work contained in the review. Again, no less than in the case of Cairns, Jennett and Sloane, and given the prominence of the review, this is telling.

There have been other more recent surveys since the advent of dedicated sports economics journals, which provide a retrospective mainly on the period prior to that advent and these tend to confirm what I have argued so far. At the time of writing, the last survey article to focus primarily on the period prior to the advent of dedicated sports economics journals was titled 'Sports attendance: A survey of the literature 1973–2007'. Villar and Guerrero (2009) surveyed 80 papers, 59 of which were published before the advent of the Journal of Sports Economics in 2000. The 60th paper in the survey is by Schmidt and Berri in the second volume of the Journal of Sports Economics in 2001. According to Villar and Guerrero, since 1973:

> researchers only make estimations that follow the standard model of economic theory … the normal practice has been to specify a one equation model of demand using attendance as the dependent variable. (Villar & Guerrero, 2009, pp. 116 and 126)

THE ADVENT OF DEDICATED SPORTS ECONOMICS JOURNALS

As noted in the introduction the Sports Management Review was established in 1998 and this was followed by Journal of Sports Economics in 2000. These catered exclusively for research centred on sports management and sports economics. These journals recognised implicitly and explicitly the need for greater breadth. The Sports Management Review described itself as 'multidisciplinary' and the editorial in the first issue of Journal of Sports Economics makes clear that the journal seeks to embrace a broad and eclectic range of issues that bring together economic theory, business, finance, history, law and politics, and use of different methods including case studies (Kahane et al., 2000). This implicitly opened the journal to an interest in social context and began a gradual conceptual shift. Work from sociology, anthropology, psychology, marketing and political science eventually began to mix with traditional management science and economics. It is important, however, to keep in mind that being open to work from many disciplines does not guarantee equal voice, or that work from several disciplines is compatible or actually integrated. Without a clear sense of how this might be achieved, often the outcome is lack of integration, juxtaposition of work, appropriation of concepts and dominance of some particular way of doing things. As the previous reference to George Stigler and economic imperialism should indicate, economics is quite different in its approach to other disciplines and is resistant to change in its fundamental concepts and methods and this remains the case even in interdisciplinary contexts.

In any case, the advent of dedicated journals led to a significant increase in interest in attendance demand across a range of disciplines, and this has offered the prospect of different perspectives with greater acknowledgement of the social dynamic of demand.[12] What has been less evident is methodological reflection among economists and integration of

---

[12] Note, it may be possible to introduce dummy variables, proxies and simulations as techniques to attempt to allow for some element of diversity or heterogeneity. It is, however, highly arguable whether this is capable of capturing novelty, change and genuine difference. This has been a longstanding issue in economics. Controlling for something, for example, creates well-behaved data which presupposes a stable data-generating process which in turn assumes a known amount of diversity and a stable source. This is problematic.

perspectives from other disciplines. Initially, little changed in the contribution of economists.

While there has been a significant increase in interest in attendance demand, this was not immediately the case in the Sports Management Review. An examination of the early contents elicits only two articles on attendance demand in the first ten volumes. The first was focussed on 'fanship' and used a survey method that was designed to measure fan satisfaction (Hill & Green, 2000). This paper was explicitly interdisciplinary but did not include any formal economic theorising. The second paper focussed on psychological measurement of motivation for attendance, but simply uses the term attendance demand and does not interrogate or develop the concept (Mahony et al., 2002).

As noted, the Journal of Sports Economics was from the outset open to a broad range of disciplines and perspectives. The journal's first article was written by Simon Rottenberg and, like his first paper in 1956, discusses the institutional arrangements of the sports industry and its key drivers. It is not an exercise in formal economic modelling. The first volume contains few formal economics papers. However, this was not to remain the case over the first few years of the journal. Moreover, while one can readily say the journal has been highly successful in terms of developing the field of sports economics and securing an outlet for publication of material devoted to it, it is fair to say that the work published in its pages on attendance demand was initially indistinguishable from earlier work and this remained the case until around 2008.

The first paper published on attendance demand in the journal was titled 'Competitive Balance and Attendance: The Case of Major League Baseball' (Schmidt & Berri, 2001). This makes the claim that a firm should seek to maximise profits but that this may be compromised by win-maximisation objectives. Models which focus on the demand function within theory of the firm implicitly incorporate versions of the standard economic agent, subject to minor modification. This was indicative of what followed in subsequent papers. For example, the most cited article on attendance in the journal, 'The determinants of football attendance revisited: empirical evidence from the Spanish football league' (Garcia & Rodriguez, 2002), clearly states estimation of a demand equation is the usual approach and builds on standard methods. The paper uses proxies and dummies to allow for heterogeneity, but the underlying concept is a standard agent.

Overall, there is an observable convergence of methods applied as the number of articles written on attendance increased across the first decade of the journal's existence. This is not surprising if one thinks that little had changed outside of sports economics in the training of economists. The first decade of the new millennium may be just after the high point of 'formalism' in economics and may coincide with what is sometimes termed 'the empirical turn', but economics remained quite distinct among the social sciences and still wedded to its core concepts and methods.[13] For example, a content analysis conducted by Mondello and Pedersen in 2003 concluded that in the first two years of the journal's life 94% of articles published used quantitative methods. For example, in an article titled 'New issues in attendance demand' (Forrest & Simmons, 2006), a tobit estimation technique is used. Tobit modelling is underpinned by statistical normality (see Amemiya, 1973). This assumes a rational agent and by extension a concept of demand that accords with rational choice theory. The method and the agent go together.

One might argue then that despite the good intentions of the editors of Journal of Sports Economics, there was not, at least initially, a great deal of change from the situation previously described. If we return to terminology we introduced earlier, then one might argue that a concept of agency that presupposes atomism remained the benchmark and the frameworks and methods used presupposed constant conjunctions. As critics also note, this is a legacy of positivism that has survived far longer than any explicit adherence to positivism and has continued despite that many economists today are not wedded explicitly to a strict positive-normative divide.[14] Economists are rarely exposed to philosophy of science or take courses in methodology or history of economic thought and so are not being equipped when trained as an economist to think about this set of issues.

---

[13] Note: there are different positions on the degree of diversity and progress indicated by the 'empirical turn' and the proliferation of modelling strategies. For discussion, some criticism but broadly positive treatments, see, for example, Angrist and Pischke (2010); Coyle (2021); Rodrik (2015). For a slightly different take on prospects, see Colander (2005); Davis (2006).

[14] For critics this invokes a set of issues regarding the implicit 'ontology' of theory and methods used. The main claim is that every approach has at least an implicit ontology since this is built into any attempt to describe, explain or understand the world. If implicit, then the ontology is not subject to proper scrutiny and problems may persist. There is, therefore, a need for debate and this is also the case for sports economics.

The Breakout Period from 2008

As noted in the introduction, around 2008 there was some sign of more significant change in the state of affairs described so far. For example, 'Does television crowd out spectators?' (Allan & Roy, 2008) clearly states that work undertaken on the impact of television coverage does not arrive at a consensus regarding determinants and the article applies a novel estimation method. While this article does not discuss sociality from around 2008, the concept of competitive balance came into use and there was recognition that gender and race affected attendance demand. Institutions and social structure became part of the language of demand. In 'The impact of postseason restructuring on the competitive balance and fan demand in Major League Baseball' (Lee, 2009), the author considers the impact of uncertainty and highlights the shift in attendees' perception when competition goes to postseason games. This is innovative.

After 2008, various social or contextual factors affecting attendance demand are incorporated in articles in Journal of Sports Economics. These include the impact of strikes (Gitter & Rhoads, 2010), consumer discrimination (Yamamura, 2011), rising stars (Gitter & Rhoads, 2011), tournament significance (Feddersen & Rott, 2011) and star power (Ormiston, 2014). In any case if one peruses Loyland and Ringstad (2009), Iho and Heikkila (2010), and Lemke et al. (2010) these all stick closely to the standard microeconomic treatment of attendance demand.[15] In the pages of Journal of Sports Economics, the economic agent did not change as much as one might at first think. Table 2.1 categorises all papers published in the journal between 2000 and 2022 that deal with attendance demand.

The period to 2008 follows the format previously discussed. It should also be noted that the frequency of publication on the subject is also quite variable. Thirteen papers on the subject were published between 2013 and 2022 of which only four were explicitly standard economic treatments of the issue.[16] Others addressed star quality (2016, 2017, 2018a, 2018b, 2020), scheduling (2019), weather (2020) and tournament design (2014, 2021).

---

[15] Lemke et al. (2010) claim to have included the most complete set of explanatory variables in the literature. There remains a focus on predictive power. Authors proceed to outline the usual mainstream theory of demand, focusing on the individual agent and economic interactions, identifying price, income, expectation and population as the main defining constraints on demand for goods and services in the sports industry.

[16] Note: this counts only papers mainly focused on attendance.

Table 2.1 The development of the demand concept in the Journal of Sports Economics, 2000–2022

Volume/ issue	Title of paper	Methodological approach	Explicit/ implicit use of the mainstream conceptual model of demand	Discussion of 'social' influences
3/1	'The Determinants of Football Match Attendance Revisited: Empirical Evidence from the Spanish Football League'	Estimation of demand equation	Explicit	No
3/4	'Interleague Play and Baseball Attendance'	Estimation of demand equation	Implicit	No
5/4	'Uncertainty of Outcome and Super 12 Rugby Union Attendance: Application of a General-to-Specific Modeling Strategy'	Estimation of demand using OLS/GETS modelling	Implicit	No
6/1	'Attendance at County Cricket: An Economic Analysis'	Estimation of demand function—OLS/ Tobit	Explicit	No
6/2	'An Evaluation of the Relationship Between Hispanics and Major League Soccer'	Estimation of demand function	Explicit	Yes—race
6/3	'How Long a Honeymoon? The Effect of New Stadiums on Attendance in Major League Baseball'	Estimation of demand equation	Explicit	No
6/3	'Baseball Strikes and Demand for Attendance'	Estimation of demand equation	Explicit	No
7/2	'Decline of Attendance in the Korean Professional Baseball League: The Major League Effects'	Estimation of demand equation	Explicit	No

(*continued*)

Table 2.1 (continued)

Volume/ issue	Title of paper	Methodological approach	Explicit/ implicit use of the mainstream conceptual model of demand	Discussion of 'social' influences
7/3	'New Issues in Attendance Demand—The Case of the English Football League'	Panel regression model	Explicit	No
7/4	'Stationarity and MLB Attendance Analysis'	Breakpoint analysis	Explicit	No
8/1	'An Analysis of Attendance at MLB Spring Training Games'	Estimation of demand function—Tobit	Explicit	No
8/6	'Competitive Balance and Game Attendance in MLB'	Multiple regression model—MLE	Explicit	No
9/1	'Impact of Overwhelming Joy on Consumer Demand: The Case of a Soccer World Cup Victory'	Estimation of demand function—OLS/ Tobit	Explicit	Yes— collective euphoria
9/6	'Does Television Crowd-Out Spectators? New Evidence from the Scottish Premier League'	Spectator characteristics— augmented fixed effects model	Implicit	No
10/1	'Analyzing the Relationship Between Team Success and MLB Attendance with GARCH Effects'	GARCH model	Implicit	No
10/3	'The Impact of Postseason Restructuring on the Competitive Balance and Fan Demand in Major League Baseball'	Breakpoint analysis	Explicit	No
10/6	'On the Price and Income Sensitivity of the Demand for Sports: Has Linder's Disease Become More Serious?'	Estimation of demand function—Tobit	Explicit	No

(continued)

Table 2.1 (continued)

Volume/ issue	Title of paper	Methodological approach	Explicit/ implicit use of the mainstream conceptual model of demand	Discussion of 'social' influences
11/2	'Impact of Advance Ticket Sales on Attendance'	Estimation of demand function—OLS	Explicit	No
11/3	'MLB Attendance—2007'	Estimation of demand function—fixed effects	Explicit	No
11/6	'Determinants of Minor League Baseball Attendance'	Estimation of demand function	Implicit	No
12/1	'Game Information, Local Heroes, and Their Effect on Attendance: The Case of the Japanese Baseball League'	Estimation of demand function	Explicit	No
12/2	'Soccer Attendees' Preferences for Facilities: An Application of the Discrete Choice Experiment'	Discrete choice experiment— willingness to pay. Logit estimation	Implicit	No
12/3	'Top Prospects and Minor League Baseball Attendance'	Estimation of demand function	Implicit	No
13/1	'Take Me Out to the Yakyushiai: Determinants of Attendance at Nippon Professional Baseball Games'	Estimation of demand function	Explicit	No
13/4	'Game Attendance and Outcome Uncertainty in the National Hockey League'	Estimation of demand function	Implicit	No
13/5	'Major League Baseball Attendance and the Role of Fantasy Baseball'	Estimation of demand function	Implicit	No

(continued)

Table 2.1 (continued)

Volume/ issue	Title of paper	Methodological approach	Explicit/ implicit use of the mainstream conceptual model of demand	Discussion of 'social' influences
14/4	'Football Frenzy: The Effect of the 2011 World Cup on Women's Professional Soccer League Attendance'	Estimation of demand equation	Implicit	Yes— collective euphoria
15/4	'Attendance Effects of Star Pitchers in Major League Baseball'	Estimation of demand equation	Implicit	No
15/5	'Major League Baseball Attendance: Long-Term Analysis Using Factor Models'	Estimation of demand equation—fixed effects	Implicit	No
17/4	'The Effect of Star Quality on Attendance Demand: The Case of the National Basketball Association'	Estimation of demand equation— censored regression model (Tobit)	Explicit	No
18/3	'The Effect of Marquee Players on Sports Demand: The Case of U.S. Major League Soccer'	Estimation of demand equation	Explicit	No
18/6	'Beer Availability and College Football Attendance: Evidence from Mid-Major Conferences'	Estimation of demand equation	Implicit	Yes—various factors
19/1	'Spectator Demand, Uncertainty of Results, and Public Interest: Evidence from the English Premier League'	Cross-sectional time series (panel) regression model	Implicit	No

(continued)

Table 2.1 (continued)

Volume/ issue	Title of paper	Methodological approach	Explicit/ implicit use of the mainstream conceptual model of demand	Discussion of 'social' influences
19/1	'The Impact of the Soccer Schedule on TV Viewership and Stadium Attendance: Evidence from the Belgian Pro League'	Discrete choice model; conditional logit model	Implicit	No
19/3	'Sellout, Blackout, or Get Out: The Impacts of the 2012 Policy Change on TV Blackouts and Attendance in the NFL'	Logit model—restricted	Implicit	No
19/4	'The Demand for Football in Portugal: New Insights on Outcome Uncertainty'	Two-stage least squares and two-stage tobit estimator	Explicit	No
19/4	'Common Factors in Major League Baseball Game Attendance'	Panel data model	Implicit	No
19/5	'Empty Seats or Empty Threats? Examining the Effects of the 1994–1995 and 2004–2005 Lockouts on Attendance and Revenue in the National Hockey League'	Estimation of demand equation	Implicit	No
19/7	'Team-Level Time Series Analysis in MLB, the NBA, and the NHL: Attendance and Outcome Uncertainty'	Break point analysis	Implicit	No
20/3	'Substitution in Sports: The Case of Lower Division Football Attendance'	Fixed effects panel regressions	Implicit	No
20/4	'Football Spectator No-Show Behaviour'	Panel data regression	Implicit	No

(*continued*)

Table 2.1 (continued)

Volume/ issue	Title of paper	Methodological approach	Explicit/ implicit use of the mainstream conceptual model of demand	Discussion of 'social' influences
21/1	'Competitive Intensity, Fans' Expectations, and Match-Day Tickets Sold in the Italian Football Serie A, 2012–2015'	Estimation of demand equation	Explicit	No
21/2	'The Effect of Superstars on Game Attendance: Evidence from the NBA'	Censored normal estimator—MLE model	Implicit	No
21/3	'Are Fair Weather Fans Affected by Weather? Rainfall, Habit Formation, and Live Game Attendance'	(Rainfall augmented) habit formation attendance model	No	Yes—habitual behaviour
21/4	'Impacts of Performance-Enhancing Drug Suspensions on the Demand for Major League Baseball'	Estimation of demand equation	Explicit	Yes—social conformity/ deviance
21/6	'Boys in the Booth: The Impact of Announcer Gender on Audience Demand'	Experimental method	Implicit	Yes—gender factors
21/7	'The Demand for the Characteristics of Football Matches: A Hedonic Price Approach'	Hedonic price function—two stage AIDS estimation of demand	Explicit	No
21/7	'The Private Benefit of Public Funding: The FIFA World Cup, UEFA European Championship, and Attendance at Host Country League Soccer'	Index formation; estimation of demand change	No	No

(*continued*)

Table 2.1 (continued)

Volume/ issue	Title of paper	Methodological approach	Explicit/ implicit use of the mainstream conceptual model of demand	Discussion of 'social' influences
21/8	'League Ranking Mobility Affects Attendance: Evidence from European Soccer Leagues'	Panel regression model	No	No
22/5	'The Effect of League Design on Spectator Attendance: A Regression Discontinuity Design Approach'	Quasi-experimental approach—sharp regression discontinuity design	Implicit	No
23/5	'Where to Go Next? Examining the Effect of Franchise Expansion and Location on Game-Level Attendance in Major League Soccer'	Panel data estimation—OLS	Implicit	Yes—habit, rivalry

GETS is a modelling technique, General to Specific

However, while there has been a greater openness regarding the determinants of demand, there has been relatively little change in the underlying methodological framing. For example, many articles made passing mention of psychological and sociological factors, especially 'fan loyalty', but none of the papers discussed what this might mean for the nature of the agent. The treatment of the agent has not been wholly different and often the main innovation has taken the form of loosening or relaxing of assumptions. There are no papers that take issue with the received construction of the economic agent or that set out to discuss the issue of atomism or the attraction of a more social alternative. There has been no debate along these lines. Nor have later survey essays used the opportunity to highlight the need for this. For example, 'Stadium attendance demand research: a scoping review' is clearly not set up to achieve this purpose (Schreyer & Ansari, 2022). It is comprehensive in date range, covering the complete period from 1956 onwards, but its role is clearly not to challenge or provoke the field.[17]

CONCLUSION AND THE CHANGED SCENE

It seems deeply ironic that sport in Western popular culture is heralded as the domain in which we learn about life and yet the economic agent applied to sport mainly assumes away what it is that makes us human. The sociality of sport seems singularly unsuited to the treatment appropriated from mainstream microeconomics and it is highly arguable whether minor modifications to that approach are sufficient. There is a debate to be had here that is not being had and that should be clear from the material I have presented. There is also great scope for alternatives. Alternatives have been few and research scarce.

Two papers provide some indication of significant difference. Neither is published in *Journal of Sports Economics* and neither is the last word on the subject we have raised here. The article 'Determinants of Individual Consumption on Sports Attendance in Spain' (Lera-López et al., 2011) published in *International Journal of Sport Finance* begins from a familiar statement:

> [b]oth approaches assume that individual's consumption decisions are aimed at maximising their utility subject to budget and time constraints … the demand for which reflects the trade-off between the utility derived from the consumption of goods and the opportunity cost of an hour of sport … utility depends on the amount of goods consumed, whereas in Becker's approach, preferences are a function of commodities produced by the household using time and goods. (Lera-López et al., 2011, p. 206)

However, the authors go on to consider other approaches to demand and specifically highlight alternatives to mainstream economics in the form of 'heterodox' perspectives.[18] They draw attention to the work of the

---

[17] For a recent survey not published in *Journal of Sports Economics*, see Johnson and Fort (2022). This follows a similar format to that discussed.

[18] Note: heterodox economics is a collective term for schools of thought that do not fit easily into the contemporary mainstream. There is some dispute regarding what schools fall into the category and there is some degree of debate about what unites them. For example, is it merely criticism of fundamental assumptions common to the 'mainstream' or do they share some positive characteristics? The term mainly refers to Post-Keynesian and Original Institutional economics but can extend to feminist economics, ecological economics, sometimes Austrian economics and others. For categorisation see Dequech (2012); for history see Lee (2010).

Post-Keynesian Marc Lavoie on consumer research and economic psy-chology (Lavoie, 2004). Post-Keynesian theory is particularly focused on uncertainty and endogeneity and has a branch of theory that is particularly interested in the role of institutions in conditioning agency and in the interdependency of decisions. This at least holds at the possibility of explicit treatment of sociality in economics. According to Lavoie:[19]

> [d]ecision preference are not made independently of other agents. A house-hold's pattern of consumption will reflect the lifestyle of the other house-holds that constitute its social reference group (Lavoie, 2004, p. 647)

In a subsequent paper titled 'Sports spectatorship in Spain: Attendance and consumption' (Lera-López et al., 2012) published in *European Sport Management Quarterly*, the authors again begin with comment on Becker's approach but in this case turn to the work of Paul Downward (2007).[20] Downward's name appears in the original editorial launching the *Journal of Sports Economics*, and over the years he has gone on to be a prominent figure in the field, an accomplished econometrician, but also an advocate of heterodox economics. The authors again highlight the inter-dependence of agents and the need to think carefully about what is at issue.

Clearly, there is great scope to explore an alternative concept of atten-dance demand for sporting events. One possible way to think about this is to situate socialised demand to a more complex socialised consumer. If sport attendance *is* recognised as a shared activity, then the agent is socialised and not atomistic. How might this agent be more appropriately conceptualised, situated and investigated?

References

Allan, G., & Roy, G. (2008). Does television crowd out spectators? *Journal of Sports Economics, 9*(6), 592–605.

Amemiya, T. (1973). Regression analysis when the dependant variable is truncated normal. *Econometrica, 41*(6), 997–1016.

[19] Note: while Lera-López et al. (2011) appear to be the first paper recognising social aspects of agency for our purposes, there are recognitions outside of the discipline of eco-nomics, mainly in the marketing sphere, with numerous models that include socialised con-sumption factors, for example Macdonald et al. (2002).

[20] Downward's paper focusses on sports participation, not sports event attendance, and therefore is not included in this literature review.

Angrist, J., & Pischke, J. (2010). The credibility revolution in empirical economics: How better research design is taking the con out of econometrics. *Journal
of Economic Perspectives, 24*(2), 3–30.

Arnsperger, C., & Varoufakis, Y. (2006). What is neoclassical economics? *Real-
World Economics Review, 38*, 2–12. http://www.paecon.net/PAEReview/
wholeissues/issue38.pdf

Bhaskar, R. (2008). *A realist theory of science.* Verso.

Blaug, M. (1992). *The methodology of economics* (2nd ed.). Cambridge
University Press.

Blaug, M. (2003). The formalist revolution of the 1950s. *Journal of the History of
Economic Thought, 25*(2), 145–156.

Borland, J., & MacDonald, R. (2003). Demand for sport. *Oxford Review of
Economic Policy, 19*(1), 478–502.

Boylan, T., & O'Gorman, O. (2007). Axiomatization and formalism in economics. *Journal of Economic Surveys, 21*(3), 426–446.

Cairns, J., Jennett, N., & Sloane, P. (1986). The economics of professional team
sports: A survey of theory and evidence. *Journal of Economic Studies,
13*(1), 3–80.

Cartwright, N. (2007). *Hunting causes and using them: Approaches in philosophy
and economics.* Cambridge University Press.

Colander, D. (2005). The future of economics: The appropriately educated in
pursuit of the knowable. *Cambridge Journal of Economics, 29*(6), 927–941.

Coyle, D. (2021). *Cogs and monsters: What economics is, and what it should be.*
Princeton University Press.

Davis, J. B. (2003). *The theory of the individual in economics: Identity and value.*
Routledge.

Davis, J. B. (2006). The turn in economics: Neoclassical dominance to mainstream pluralism? *Journal of Institutional Economics, 2*(1), 1–20.

Davis, J. B. (2011). *Individuals and identity in economics.* Cambridge
University Press.

Dequech, D. (2007). Neoclassical, mainstream, orthodox and heterodox economics. *Journal of Post Keynesian Economics, 30*(2), 279–302.

Dequech, D. (2012). Post Keynesianism, heterodoxy and mainstream economics.
Review of Political Economy, 24(2), 353–368.

Dow, S. (1997). Mainstream economic methodology. *Cambridge Journal of
Economics, 21*(1), 73–93.

Downward, P. (2007). Exploring the economic choice to participate in sport:
Results from the 2002 general household survey. *International Review of
Applied Economics, 21*(5), 633–653.

Feddersen, A., & Rott, A. (2011). Determinants of demand for televised live football: Features of the German National Football Team. *Journal of Sports
Economics, 12*(3), 352–369.

Forrest, D., & Simmons, R. (2006). New issues in attendance demand. *Journal of Sports Economics, 7*(3), 247–266.

Fullbrook, E. (2002a). Why intersubjectivity? In E. Fullbrook (Ed.), *Intersubjectivity in economics—Agents and structures* (pp. 1–10). Routledge.

Fullbrook, E. (Ed.). (2002b). *Intersubjectivity in economics.* Routledge.

Garcia, J., & Rodriguez, P. (2002). The determinants of football attendance revisited: Empirical evidence from the Spanish football league. *Journal of Sports Economics, 3*(1), 18–38.

Gitter, S. R., & Rhoads, T. A. (2010). Determinants of minor league baseball attendance. *Journal of Sports Economics, 11*(6), 614–628.

Gitter, S. R., & Rhoads, T. A. (2011). Top prospect and minor league baseball attendance. *Journal of Sports Economics, 12*(3), 341–351.

Groff, R. (2008). Introduction: Realism about causality. In R. Groff (Ed.), *Revitalizing causality: Realism about causality in philosophy and social science* (pp. 1–10). Routledge.

Groff, R. (2017). Causal mechanisms and the philosophy of causation. *Journal for the Theory of Social Behaviour, 47*(3), 286–305.

Hamilton, D. (2018). *Going to the match: The passion for football.* Hodder and Stoughton.

Hill, B., & Green, B. C. (2000). Repeat attendance as a function of involvement, loyalty, and the sportscape across three football contexts. *Sport Management Review, 3*(2), 145–162.

Hodgson, G. (2007). Meanings of methodological individualism. *Journal of Economic Methodology, 14*(2), 211–226.

Hodgson, G. M. (2004). *The evolution of institutional economics: Agency, structure and Darwinism in American institutionalism.* Routledge.

Iho, A., & Heikkila, J. (2010). Impact of advanced ticket sales on attendance in the Finnish football league. *Journal of Sports Economics, 11*(2), 214–226.

Johnson, S., & Fort, R. (2022). Match outcome uncertainty and sports fan demand: An agnostic review and the standard economic theory of sports leagues. *International Journal of Empirical Economics, 1*(2), 2250007.

Kahane, L. H., Idson, T. L., & Staudohar, P. D. (2000). Editorial: Introducing a new journal. *Journal of Sports Economics, 1*(1), 1–10.

Karni, E. (2016). Savage's subjective expected utility model. In M. Vernengo, E. Caldentey, & B. Rosser Jr. (Eds.), *The new Palgrave dictionary of economics.* Palgrave Macmillan. Online continuously updating version. https://doi.org/1 0.1057/978-1-349-95121-5_2467-1

Lavoie, M. (2004). Post Keynesian consumer theory: Potential synergies with consumer research and economic psychology. *Journal of Economic Psychology, 25*(5), 639–649.

Lawson, T. (1997). *Economics and reality.* Routledge.

Lawson, T. (2003). *Reorienting economics.* Routledge.

Lawson, T. (2015a). *Essays on the nature and state of modern economics*. Routledge.

Lawson, T. (2015b). *The nature and state of modern economics*. Routledge.

Lee, F. (2010). *A history of heterodox economics*. Routledge.

Lee, H. L. (2009). The impact of postseason restructuring on the competitive balance and fan demand in Major League Baseball. *Journal of Sports Economics, 10*(3), 219–235.

Lemke, R. J., Leonard, M., & Tlhokwane, K. (2010). Estimating attendance demand at major league Baseball games for the 2007 season. *Journal of Sports Economics, 11*(3), 316–348.

Lera-López, F., Ollo-López, A., & Rapún-Gárate, M. (2012). Sports spectatorship in Spain: Attendance and consumption. *European Sport Management Quarterly, 12*(3), 265–289.

Lera-López, F., Rapún-Gárate, M., & Suárez, M. J. (2011). Determinants of individual consumption on sports attendance in Spain. *International Journal of Sport Finance, 6*(3), 204–221.

Loyland, K., & Ringstad, V. (2009). On the price and income sensitivity of the demand for sports: Has Linders disease become more serious? *Journal of Sports Economics, 10*(6), 601–618.

Macdonald, M. A., Milne, G. R., & Hong, J. (2002). Motivational factors for evaluating sport spectator and participant markets. *Sport Marketing Quarterly, 11*(2), 100–113.

Machina, M. J. (2008). Expected utility hypothesis. In S. N. Durlauf & L. E. Blume (Eds.), *The new Palgrave dictionary of economics* (2nd ed.). Palgrave Macmillan.

Mahony, D. F., Nakazawa, M., Funk, D. C., James, J. D., & Gladden, J. M. (2002). Motivational factors influencing the behaviour of J. League spectators. *Sport Management Review, 5*(1), 1–24.

Mäki, U. (Ed.). (2001). *The economic world view: Studies in the ontology of economics*. Cambridge University Press.

Mason, P., & Shan, H. (2017). A valence-free definition of sociality as any violation of inter-individual independence. *Proceedings of the Royal Society, B., 284*, 20170948.

Morgan, J. (2016a). Critical realism as a social ontology for economics. In S. Lee & B. Cronin (Eds.), *Handbook of research methods and applications in heterodox economics* (pp. 15–34). Edward Elgar.

Morgan, J. (Ed.). (2016b). *What is neoclassical economics?* Routledge.

Neale, W. C. (1964). The peculiar economics of professional sports: A contribution to the theory of the firm in sporting competition and in market competition. *The Quarterly Journal of Economics, 78*(1), 1–14.

Noll, R. G. (1974). Attendance and Price setting. In R. G. Noll (Ed.), *Government and the sports business* (pp. 115–158). The Brookings Institution.

Ormiston, R. (2014). Attendance effects of star pitchers in Major League Baseball. *Journal of Sports Economics, 15*(4), 338–364.

Rodrik, D. (2015). *Economics rules: Why economics works, when it fails and how to tell the difference.* Oxford University Press.

Rottenberg, S. (1956). The baseball players labor market. *Journal of Political Economy, 64*(3), 242–258.

Samuelson, P. A. (1937). A note on the measurement of utility. *The Review of Economic Studies, 4*(2), 155–161.

Samuelson, P. A. (1938a). A note on the pure theory of consumer's behaviour. *Economica, 5*(17), 61–71.

Samuelson, P. A. (1938b). A note on the pure theory of consumer's behaviour: An addendum. *Economica, 5*(19), 353–354.

Samuelson, P. A. (1938c). The empirical implications of utility analysis. *Econometrica, 6*(4), 344–356.

Samuelson, P. A. (1938d). The numerical representation of ordered classifications of the concept of utility. *Review of Economic Studies, 6*(1), 65–70.

Schmidt, M. B., & Berri, D. J. (2001). Competitive balance and attendance: The case of Major League Baseball. *Journal of Sports Economics, 2*(2), 145–167.

Schofield, J. A. (1983). Performance and attendance at professional team sports. *Journal of Sport Behavior, 6*(4), 196–206.

Schreyer, D., & Ansari, P. (2022). Stadium attendance demand research: A scoping review. *Journal of Sports Economics, 23*(6), 749–788.

Sloane, P. J. (1971). The economics of professional football: The football club as utility maximiser. *Scottish Journal of Political Economy, 18*(2), 121–146.

Statista. (2022a). Professional sports overview. Last viewed 1st October 2023. https://www.statista.com/markets/409/topic/627/professional-sports/#overview

Statista. (2022b). Total regular season attendance of selected sports leagues worldwide in 2019. Last viewed 1st October 2023. https://www.statista.com/statistics/1120142/total-sports-attendance-by-league/

Stigler, G. (1984). Economics: The Imperial science? *The Scandinavian Journal of Economics, 86*(3), 301–313.

Villar, J. G., & Guerrero, P. R. (2009). Sports attendance: A survey of the literature 1973–2007. *Rivista Di Diritto Ed Economia Dello Sport, 5*(2), 111–151.

Weintraub, R. (2002). *How economics became a mathematical science.* Duke University Press.

Yamamura, E. (2011). Game information, local heroes, and their effect on attendance: The case of the Japanese baseball league. *Journal of Sports Economics, 12*(1), 20–35.

CHAPTER 3

Missing Links: Towards a Theory of Social Economic Agency for Sports Attendance

Abstract In this chapter I address the need for debate regarding the standard economic agent presupposed or used in sports attendance demand theory and research. I first set out a participant observation ethnographic account of 'a day at the football'. This provides a contrast in order to ask the question, 'is it reasonable to think that the person who attended a sports event of the kind described becomes some version of the standard economic agent at the point of purchase of the ticket that secures attendance?' I then discuss in detail the issues that this raises regarding a social agent and suggest that sports economics is one side of a more basic divide in its approach to economics. Finally, I explore some possible concepts and resources for 'the other side of the divide'.

Keywords Sports economics • Attendance demand • Economic agent • Shared agency

INTRODUCTION

As I have previously argued, a survey of the available literature in sports economics on sports attendance indicates that prior to the establishment of dedicated sports economics journals at the turn of the millennium, the standard economic agent drawn from neoclassical economics was either

© The Author(s), under exclusive license to Springer Nature
Switzerland AG 2024
J. Embery, *Attendance Demand in Sports Economics*, Palgrave Pivots
in Sports Economics,
https://doi.org/10.1007/978-3-031-60040-1_3

deployed or presupposed in the vast majority of published research.[1] While subsequent research exhibits some diversity, the standard economic agent has remained the benchmark. This rational agent makes isolated *individual* decisions in a narrow calculative fashion intended to maximise utility and does so based on abundant information regarding consumption. Methodologists refer to this isolation as atomism.[2] Adoption of this agent is odd, since sports attendance is quintessentially social.

There are, however, many reasons why this agent has been adopted. Sports economists are educated and trained as economists and so absorb the same basic conceptual toolkit and canon of theory and methods as their colleagues. The mainstream economic agent is assumed to be universally applicable so it may not be immediately obvious to sports economists that the mismatch matters. Moreover, few economists are exposed to history of economic thought and philosophy and methodology of economics during their education and may lack the tools to consider the issues that these provide. Instead, the skills that are encouraged by a mainstream economics education involve model building and analysis and this is easier to do with an atomistic optimising decisionmaker. Others working in the field of sports attendance who are not economists may lack the understanding of what underpins theories and models drawn from economics and thus may not feel able to contest published research. Finally, once theory and methods embed, it becomes easier to publish if one conforms to 'the discourse'.[3]

---

[1] Note: throughout the chapter I switch between use of 'I' and 'we' as appropriate to context. Throughout the chapter I mainly refer to attendance demand, but the issues apply more generally to demand for spectation which may or may not be in person and different scholars who I draw on for the literature use a variety of terms.

[2] Atomism has several related meanings in philosophy. For various early Greek philosophers it refers to the claim that reality is composed of fundamental units. In the seventeenth century the focus turned to the inability to observe these units and what that implied about what we can know. Later, Bertrand Russell introduced the concept of 'logical atomism' to refer to elementary propositions and this influenced Ludwig Wittgenstein. In economics, however, the main use of the term (the one I am using) is to refer to isolation from influences of a base unit—the atom. The concept is closely associated with the language of open and closed systems (see Dow, 2012, pp. 149–153 and also later in this chapter). On the different meanings of atomism in philosophy, see Chalmers (2019); Proops (2022).

[3] There is a lot of research and comment discussing the sociology of knowledge of economics, which makes the point that it is unusual among the social sciences: the mainstream of the discipline is more mathematical, unified in its approach to what is 'economics' and how it is 'done' and hierarchical than politics or sociology. Marion Fourcade is very well known on this. Others who have discussed the issues include Arjo Klamer and David Colander (who explore the training and attitudes of economists and how they self-identify), and Andrew Mearman and colleagues who explore the limits imposed on the curriculum and teaching initiatives in the UK. See, for example, Mearman et al. (2018); Fourcade et al. (2015); Klamer and Colander (1990).

What all the above suggests is that there is a debate to be had here that is not being had. Towards this end, in this chapter I explore the sociality of sports attendance in order to highlight the difference this makes. The intention is to provide a background argument for an alternative theorisation of the *social* economic agent for sports attendance, but the purpose of the chapter is not to provide that alternative theorisation—that remains to be done. The chapter proceeds in six main sections.

In Sect. 'A Day at the Gallery' I begin by setting the scene. I highlight how I came to question the standard economic agent used in attendance demand for sports economics. In Sect. 'A Day at the Football' I provide an ethnographic participant observation account of attendance at a football match. This makes it very clear that attendance is a social activity. In Sect. 'A Reminder of the Key Features of the Economic Agent' I briefly reprise the key features of the standard economic agent and the progress and limitations on progress made in developing that agent in the context of sports attendance demand. In Sect. 'What Does it Mean or What Is It Worth?' I begin from the question, does it make sense to assume that the person described in the ethnographic account becomes some version of the standard economic agent at the point of purchase of the ticket that secures attendance? I then provide a series of observations which contrasts theory and reality as a critique of the agent. I follow this in Sect. 'Three Versions of a Dividing Line' by placing the terms of debate in a broader context. Arguably, given the sociality of sports attendance, sports economics is on the wrong side of a longstanding divide in economics. In Sect. 'A Few Illustrations of the Potential of the Other Side of the Divide' I provide a selection of work from the 'other side of the divide' which illustrates the potential for a more social concept of the agent. I then conclude.

As a preliminary comment it should be undeniable that sports attendance is social since this is easily observed at any major sports event. The excitement that supporters crave is organically created as social and collective phenomena. There is synergy and amplification. The significance of this is evident when contrasted with the games broadcast from empty stadiums during the COVID-19 lockdown (Grix et al., 2021). If this chapter has an underlying theme, then it is that we should recall what we all know about sport but forget when we think like economists.

A Day at the Gallery

Let's start with a quote from the artist L. S. Lowry, known for his depiction of working-class life in the industrialised North of England in the mid-twentieth century:

> People think crowds are all the same. But they're not, you know. Everyone's different. Look! That man's got a twitch. He's got a limp. He's had too much beer … It's wonderful isn't it? The battle of life, sir. That's what it is. The battle of life. (Rosenthal, 2009, p. 183)

I came across this quote after a visit to the Lowry Gallery in Salford, Manchester. The quote is taken from a work by the art historian Tom Rosenthal and is from a conversation between Lowry and Edwin Mullins. It draws attention to a common theme in Lowry's work, the diversity of crowds. However, as Rosenthal also highlights, 'individuality is not what matters to Lowry. They are a crowd, a cluster, a congregation' (Jacobson cited in Rosenthal, 2009, p. 169). For Lowry, the important thing is that the many *become* a crowd and that crowd has a kind of everyday togetherness. This theme of community but not quite uniformity is one that will be apparent to anyone who has visited the Lowry Gallery and nowhere is it more obvious than in Lowry's well-known 1953 painting 'Going to the Match'. The painting depicts clusters and snaking lines of Lowry's trademark stick figures descending on a packed traditional open-roofed and terraced stadium. As Rosenthal observes, the painting evokes 'in its barely suppressed excitement … a huge crowd in directed and purposive motion' (Rosenthal, 2009, p. 132). Terraced houses and belching factory chimney stacks provide a backdrop to the scene and this is a stark reminder of the working-class associations of football in particular at that time.

The experience of visiting the Lowry Gallery had a similar impact on the sports journalist Duncan Hamilton to the one it had on me and he incorporates it in his recent book, pointedly titled *Going to the Match: The Passion for Football* (Hamilton, 2018). Hamilton identifies a powerful sense of working-class solidarity and humour in Lowry's pictures but is also keenly aware that modern sport has moved on since 1953. It is big business and has become a highly commodified entertainment.[4] Part of its appeal, however, is still the existence of a fan base for whom support

---

[4] Hundreds of millions attending the most popular sports leagues annually (Statista, 2022). For example, the English Premier league had in-person attendance of over 15 million fans in 2023. Global TV audiences were over 4.7 billion, with a total revenue for the 20 Premier League clubs in excess of £5.8 billion.

(rooted in attendance, spectation, etc.) has a deeper meaning and significance.[5] This is nicely captured by the sardonic humour of former Liverpool FC manager Bill Shankly, 'Some people believe football is a matter of life and death, I am very disappointed with that attitude. I can assure you it is much, much more important than that.'[6] While this quote is often misused to imply nothing else matters, it does underscore that sport takes on an importance in the life of some that has qualities that seem very far from simple transactional behaviour. This led me to reflect on my own experience of sports attendance as a useful way to provide a contrast with the standard economic agent familiar from mainstream textbooks and sports economics research.

I have been a Preston North End FC fan most of my life and have been attending matches with varying degrees of frequency for around 35 years.[7] The following is a stylised account of the events, thoughts and feeling from a typical match day during the years I was a season ticket holder at the Deepdale stadium. The year is 2018 and the match is against Swansea City. Preston was in the Championship, which used to be the first division but after the creation of the Premier League effectively became a second division to which teams could be relegated from the Premiership and from which they could be promoted. The main characters in the account are me, Michael, Paul and Chris. Michael is my brother, Paul is Michael's friend (they met in a pub through a third party and soon struck up a friendship through their mutual interest in football) and Chris is Paul's father. Chris is about 60 years old, Paul and Michael are in their late 30s, and I am 47. The account forms a type of informal ethnographic participant observation.[8] Features of it will be familiar to many who have experienced team sport attendance.

---

[5] As Rudy Meir and Don Scott note there is a potent strand of tribalism associated with professional sport which marketing can 'encourage and facilitate' (Meir & Scott, 2007).

[6] As the article in the *Daily Mirror* from which this is taken explains, however, the quote is often misused. Visit: https://www.mirror.co.uk/sport/football/news/bill-shanklys-famous-life-death-21784583.

[7] Full disclosure, I am also a Liverpool FC fan, though the two rarely if ever come into conflict.

[8] For discussion of ethnographic method in a sports context, see in *Routledge Handbook of Qualitative Research in Sports and Exercise*, especially Atkinson (2016).

A Day at the Football

Saturday is match day. We are playing Swansea. Kick-off is at 3.00 pm. Michael walks through the door at my house. We are both dressed for the occasion (replica shirts). It is just after midday. We're on schedule. There's a bacon sandwich waiting for him, already cooked. I cook, he drives. A good bacon sandwich is my contribution. We're meeting Paul and his dad Chris at 1:30 pm—at the car park at a local primary school on Blackpool Rd where we always park. It's just five-minute walk from the ground. Paul's got an 'early pass out'. This is a running joke. Paul often defers to his wife Lisa, but on match days she sometimes gives him permission to leave the house early to socialise (this leads to all kinds of gendered humour about him being 'under the thumb'). On the way to meet Paul and Chris we check the team news. It isn't good, we have key injuries, they don't. Swansea's Scottish striker is fit. Conversation revolves around the difference this makes and we share doubts about the North End defence. Swansea's striker's participation may tip the balance their way. But it isn't a foregone conclusion. We'll give them a good match.

We arrive at St Gregory's car park and Paul and Chris are already there. Parking is always difficult for games; if you arrive later than 2.00 pm there are no spaces anywhere. (The school charged £3 at the time as a small revenue stream and like many other similar sites offers some security for the cars parked there.) The school is a handy spot to beat the traffic coming out of the ground after the game, but we are not the type to leave early to beat the traffic. This is another common subject of conversation—would you leave the cinema before the end of the film—what kind of people leave before the game is finished?

Chris is impatient and wants to get a couple of pints in at the club before we go into the ground. We always go to the St Gregory's Social Club on Blackpool Rd, just next to the school. As soon as we meet up Paul and Chris seamlessly join in the conversation about the team. Pre-match conversation has a rhythm and focus and we do not need to explain the context. Chris says our defence is OK, so that's a relief, but the Swansea striker remains a concern. There are nods all round. Swansea has recently been in the Premier League and has spent some 'serious money'. North End has stuck to a tightly balanced budget. This is frustrating for many fans and Chris, as he has many times before, questions whether 'we' really want to get promoted or whether the club lack ambition and are happy to stay in the Championship. It is usually my role to take the other side in this argument and I tell him—for the umpteenth time—that the Premier League may be 'the promised land', but we shouldn't break the bank trying to get there. That would be reckless.

The club's busy and contains the usual mix of sociable young and middle-aged fans. The atmosphere is like any other match-day afternoon, a sense of expectation, loud 'banter' from some of the more boisterous young fans and a quiet sense of menace, which doesn't faze us. There are people checking us out as we come in to make sure we 'belong'. Michael and Paul have been coming here with Chris since before they turned 18. It's a bit loud for Chris, but he's happy because it's close to the ground. Every now and then team anthems and well-rehearsed familiar chants carry across the pub. Many of these use language and express sentiments we wouldn't find acceptable in any other context. I've thought it before and think it again, I wouldn't bring my young daughter in here (I do take my daughter to watch Liverpool every now and then but when we go to Anfield we stay clear of places like this and stick to quieter cafes and the Family Zone). In any case, she's not interested in North End, Championship football is not glamorous enough for her—she's not 'committed'. There are though quite a few women in the social club and at the match, but it's hard to say if this has had much of a moderating effect on behaviour. We are surrounded by the usual faces and there are nods and greetings. Like many modern clubs and pubs this one has big screens televising a constant flow of sports news and we settle under one while checking for team updates. Chris spots someone he knows (Martin) and they chat. Chris and Martin have been watching North End and coming into this club for over 30 years. There is a nervous energy slowly building.

At about quarter past two we head for Deepdale. It's a short walk and we are not alone. Deepdale is surrounded by old style terraced housing and narrow residential streets. The crowd filters towards the ground from all sides. As we get nearer the crowd thickens and we are shoulder to shoulder with others. There is a distinctive smell and sound—cheap cooking oil, frying burgers and onions, the sweet aroma of tomato sauce. Even if no one is shouting or singing (and they usually are in fits and starts), there is a background murmur of many quiet voices that combine and swell to sound like a human thunderstorm. There are people selling fanzines and memorabilia. Along one route the police corral and protect organised groups of away fans arriving from the train station or from designated coach parks. Here and there a few smaller groups of unprotected away fans merge with the throng, jackets zipped tight hiding their replica shirts, keen not to draw attention to themselves. If my eyes were closed I would still know exactly where and when I was.

To use a well-known phrase, for all four of us Deepdale is 'our happy place'. The ground is filling up quickly and the turnstiles are busy. When we get to our seats I can see that the ground is already half full. Like any team in a division below the Premiership, a full house is rare, but it should be a good crowd today. As we sit down side by side I reflect on how lucky I am this year—a season ticket became available next to the three of them. I couldn't get to games that often during the period before I moved back to Preston and didn't have a season ticket. After that I had one just in front of Michael for three years. Michael, Paul and Chris have had their season tickets since the stand became all-seater. They're roughly in the same position behind the stairwell as they were on the terrace. Chris prefers this location because he's short and the stairwell means that there are no tall people in front of him.

Every new season ticket in an existing stand has a story of loss behind it. My seat was previously occupied by Old Harry. He'd been coming to Deepdale since the 1950s (the era of Preston's greatest player, Tom Finney). For some of that time he'd been coming with his son Peter. Harry recently moved down South to live with his daughter in Bournemouth. Peter is a divorced accountant who lives somewhere near Chorley. Now Harry isn't here, Peter has stopped coming too ('It's just not the same'). As we take our seats I look around recognising some faces and names, recalling snippets of information and seeing a living archive of fan history.

The whistle blows and the first half commences. The game is like any other but only insofar as it is unique. The action drifts around the pitch and time speeds up and slows down as the game switches from lull to frenetic action. The crowd has its favourites—heroes and villains—and different players come in for special attention, well-worn songs of adulation and screams of abuse. There are members of the crowd who take on different responsibilities, initiating chants or starting handclaps. Different 'characters' in our section of the ground improvise new variations on things we've seen them do many times before. The would-be managers shout tactical advice at coaches and players and exhort them to greater effort (others shake their heads and exchange amused glances—'everyone's an expert'); the referee is accused of poor eyesight and worse judgement. Every indeterminate call is contested. There are small moments of humour, sudden moments of excitement that drag everyone out of their seats, screams of indignation, thousands of gasping intakes of breath and collective sighs of disappointment or shouts of triumph. All of this is familiar and yet all of its own. Even the misery is addictive.

The game is intense, it produces few goals, but is a close match. We dominate the first half and nick a goal from a rebound. The crowd go wild. Pent-up emotion is released in a tangle of hugs and cheers. In that moment there are no strangers in our stand, just fans whose name we don't know. This is what it means to be a football community. We could have, and should have, scored another before half-time, but waste the chance. The crowd are edgy and the half-time whistle blows. The couple two-rows-down turn around and we do what we usually do—dissect the first half. Chris is his usual pessimistic self, predicting a second half collapse, he always thinks we'll lose. Michael asks where the couple were for the last home game (their absence was noted)—it emerges they were away on holiday. Others seek the toilets or head for the half-time pies.

The game restarts and the second half flies by and then suddenly slows down. We are hanging on. Our goalkeeper has a stormer and makes at least one world-class save. Anxiety turns into sporadic hostility towards the players and our nervousness is contagious, the defence becomes shambolic. We will the minutes to tick by, concentrating as much on the clock as the game and at last the final whistle blows. The sense of relief is palpable. Players who moments before were targets are applauded off the pitch. The keeper takes a bow and we join the organised chaos as the crowd scrambles for the exits and heads for the train station, bus station and various car parks. The mood is buoyant and we reflect on the game and look forward to the next home game against Millwall. Plans are discussed and agreed. I won't see Chris and Paul again until then, but Michael will be out with Paul on Friday and the two of them and Chris are planning to go to the away game at Blackburn without me.

A Reminder of the Key Features
of the Economic Agent

Before picking out some features from the above, let's remind ourselves of the standard mainstream economic agent, that is the decisionmaker and their place in sports economics. This will be familiar to anyone who has studied 'mainstream' microeconomics.[9] The primary question an agent asks is 'is it worth it?'. This decision is made as an individual and with regard to self-interest. This in turn is translated into a utility function with a budget constraint. The agent is assumed to seek to maximise utility. The agent is rational, preferring more to less and most to least and decisions conform to transitivity (if A is preferred to B and B to C, then A is preferred to C) and are assumed to be intertemporally consistent. All necessary information to undertake decisions is available and *ex-ante* and *ex-post* utility are assumed to either coincide or converge. The agent is able to process information instantaneously and unerringly and will do so following the same procedure on every occasion. The decision is essentially a calculation and pricing and cost are its focal point.

While at a general level of theory, preferences are assumed to be 'given', and models can be specified to identify variables of interest and to test the strength of their relation to the decision. Theory and models are then developed to deal with different decision contexts and academic interest focuses on debating the degree to which given assumptions can be loosened and on developing models with different variables of interest focused on using different data and statistical techniques. In standard statistical models variables are 'separable' and the combination is 'additive'. Assessment of internal and external validity of models becomes the primary way in which findings are established and new research begins

---

[9] Note: most economic theory and models have a decisionmaker and the catch-all term for this is 'the agent', but while the standard agent is often used, it is rarely identified and summarised for the purposes of discussion. However, entries in the *New Palgrave Dictionary of Economics* (despite the title it is not a dictionary in the usual sense) provide state of the field surveys of key concepts and this includes the history of the concept of 'economic man', as well as treatment of some of the associated features and characteristics of the agent, such as 'utility' and 'transitivity'. See, for example Hargreaves-Heap and Clark (2017); Black (2017); Shafer (2017). For overview see Davis (2003).

with a literature review that itemises the headline findings regarding variables of interest in existing research.[10]

There is, of course, far greater sophistication in state of the field research over the last 50 years. As Mark Machina notes in his entry in *The New Palgrave Dictionary of Economics*, expected utility theory (EUT) has become the 'predominant descriptive and prescriptive theory of individual choice' (Machina, 2008, p. 131). In EUT, as the term literally states the agent maximises *expected* utility. EUT is a sub-branch of consumer theory and 'the expected utility model proceeds by specifying a set of objects of choice and assuming that the individual possesses a preference ordering over these objects' (Machina, 2008, p. 131). Essentially the theory combines a utility function and a preference function according to axioms which allow an optimisation procedure despite that the focal point is 'uncertain prospects' rather than 'deterministic outcomes'.[11] While the term uncertainty is used, the theory is a probabilistic approach (objective or subjective) and has carefully specified characteristics of and rules of choice. The axiomatisation and many formal proofs of axiomatisation are highly developed.[12] However, as Machina acknowledges, 'since the late 1970s there has been a revival of interest in the testing of the expected utility model; a growing body of evidence that individuals' preferences systematically depart from ... the probabilities; and the development, analysis and application of alternative models of choice ... It is fair to say that today the debate over the descriptive (and even normative) validity of the expected utility hypothesis is more extensive than it has been in over half

[10] In quantitative research, internal validity refers to the degree to which findings within the context of the study focus (i.e. its time, place, participants and subject) are justified according to recognised procedures, typically statistical and/or treatment of different variables and control groups, etc., while external validity refers to how far the findings can be generalised to other contexts (times, places, etc.).

[11] Note: clearly, this modifies any claim that an agent has complete or perfect information. Instead, they have clear preferences and a utility function and then clear rules by which they interact with either the object state of the world or the subjective state of their preferences and this allows convergence on rationally dictated optimal outcomes (though it is dangerous to generalise since EUT has so many applications and forms).

[12] Note, while there are many versions of axiomatisation there are as Machina states four main axioms: 'completeness, transitivity, [mixture] continuity and the independence Axiom' (Machina, 2008, p. 134). In addition, various developments add other well-known components such as Leonard Savage's 'sure thing principle'. The details and proofs of axioms rather than the widely acknowledged effect they have are irrelevant to my argument. For this I rely mainly on critiques from behavioural economics.

a century' (Machina, 2008, p. 137). Put simply, evidence indicates agents do not act as the theory suggests (and this, of course, is basic to behavioural economics). In any case, attendance demand often opts for a relatively simplified approach as Jeffrey Borland and Robert McDonald's highly cited survey suggests:

> The economic theory of demand for attendance at sporting events is based on a standard consumer theory model. A representative consumer is assumed to choose a consumption bundle to maximise utility, subject to a budget constraint … Existence of a budget constraint introduces a fundamental trade-off for consumers – that the opportunity cost of consuming more of one good or service is the reduction of the amounts of other goods and services that can be consumed. (Borland & MacDonald, 2003, pp. 480–481)

The starting point is, therefore, some version of a universally applicable and homogeneous, rational, well-informed, self-interested, optimising and calculative *individual* making self-regarding decisions in an isolated fashion and with a focus on pricing.[13] As I have previously argued this begins with the seminal papers of Rottenberg (1956), Neale (1964) and Sloane (1971) and while there has been some progress since then it is still the case that this 'atomistic' agent remains the benchmark. This is, for example, clearly stated in a recent retrospective in *Journal of Sports Economics*, which explicitly notes that the field has been dominated by mainstream microeconomic foundations and quantitative methods (Andreff, 2022).

Progress has taken at least five forms. First, innovative new models introducing new variables of interest. For example, the paper 'An empirical model of attendance factors at major sporting events' focuses on the role facilities play in influencing attendance (Hall et al., 2010).[14] Second, exploitation of new datasets that allow identification of differences between sub-groups of agents. For example, Hojun Sung and Hyunwoong Pyun compare attendance decisions between season ticket holders and daily ticket purchasers for the K-League I (Korean soccer premier division), modified by distance, weekend and evening game variables (Sung & Pyun, 2023). Third, focus on changes in rules which affect the underlying

---

[13] Note: while the overall context is a pricing decision, the dependent variable is attendance demand. See previous footnotes for caveats regarding 'well-informed'.

[14] Note: the purpose here is to highlight the introduction of new variables of interest. Models, of course, contain more than one variable.

attraction of sports events. For example, Johan Rewilak tests a model of the effects on attendance demand of the introduction of a 'designated player' rule in Major League soccer—the rule allowed teams to recruit and pay a star under different conditions than other players (Rewilak, 2023).[15] These first three types of innovation lead to an expanding list of possible motives, facilitators and constraints for sports attendance, but the agent within these models remains essentially the same (for a sense of these points from an earlier survey, see Borland & Macdonald, 2003).

Fourth, research-identifying behavioural bias. This follows a standard research strategy in mainstream economics. An economic agent (EUT, etc.) is used as a benchmark and then some difference between this agent in terms of expected and actual outcomes is defined as an irrationality or behavioural bias. The difference is tested using either natural experiment or laboratory conditions. For example, Candon Johnson uses the concept of 'loss aversion' to establish that expected home team losses are a driver of attendance demand in the American National Basketball Association (Johnson, 2021). This kind of work draws on a particular interpretation of the work of the founders of behavioural economics and implies but does not necessarily discuss some concept of 'bounded rationality'.[16] Fifth and finally, there is a growing body of research that identifies limitations in the usual modelling techniques ability to cope with the peculiarities of sports attendance demand. For example, there is some concern over the role that uncertainty of outcome plays in driving attendance demand and an associated concern with the interdependency of variables (see, e.g. Skrok, 2016). In the case of the fourth type of innovation, the standard economic agent is still retained despite the difference of focus and in the fifth type the problem is posed as a need for better model specification and treatment but importantly does not necessarily work with alternative concepts of agency.[17]

---

[15] The model divides variables into the DP (designated player) rule and a catch-all of other variables at the first stage of specification.

[16] Note: bounded rationality has several interpretations in behavioural economics and Daniel Kahneman, for example, did not use this term in his early work.

[17] Note: one might also draw attention to innovative work done within these constraints on television spectatorship. For example, on the role of 'emotional cues' and demand (Richardson et al., 2023); the role of 'suspense and surprise' (Bizzozero et al., 2016).

What Does It Mean or What Is It Worth?

There is an obvious question to ask here, 'is it reasonable to think that the person who attended a sports event of the kind described in the previous ethnographic participant observation section becomes some version of the standard economic agent at the point of purchase of the ticket that secures attendance?' Before considering this, let's first introduce three possible ways consumption might happen. Goods and services may be chosen individually and consumed individually, chosen individually but consumed collectively or chosen collectively and consumed collectively. The standard economic agent's focus is the first of these, but the second and third are likely more relevant to a sports attendee. Moreover, if we think of the attendee as a fan, then 'consumption' does not seem to capture what is involved. Fandom is intrinsic to who you are; it is a way of life not an act of consumption (refer to a fan as a consumer and it will likely be understood as an insult), and this surely matters for how we answer the question I began this section with.

For the standard mainstream economic agent, the driving question is 'is it worth it?' and this is focused on price as a barometer. But for a fan the logic of any decision regarding paying for attendance is typically reversed. The presumption is attend (or spectate by some other means) and one needs reasons *not* to do so. 'What are the barriers to attendance?' is a different logic than 'is it worth it?' in price terms. For a fan the question may well be 'how will I afford that?' and so a budget constraint is not irrelevant, but the driving rationale in such a circumstance is 'what do I need to do in order to be able to afford that?' and this is a very different thought process.[18] Wrapped up in it is all the commitments and experiences—the emotions and sense of self—that are exhibited on match day. A decision in these circumstances cannot be calculative in the transactional sense. For a fan 'it is not about the money'.

Furthermore, in paying for attendance one is buying a known unknown. I referred previously to 'The game is like any other but only insofar as it is unique'. Attending a sports event, especially a team sport event attended as a fan who does so regularly, is a known quantity insofar as there are familiar faces and typical components to the event, but a core appeal of competitive sport is that the outcome is unknown. It may be a shock if one

---

[18] Note: it would be inappropriate to describe this as 'opportunity cost' since this just shifts the problem to a different part of the rational decision-making process by a rational agent.

team wins 'against the odds', but the possibility of this is itself part of the appeal (a 'David and Goliath' scenario). Events in competitive team sports involve rigorous training and the development of skill sets and positional speciality, the implementation of strategies and tactics, but also reaction, errors, improvisation and the unexpected. Sport is dramatic but not tightly scripted, and while it is entertainment, attendance does not necessarily turn on how entertaining a team are or a particular game is. A team can acquire a reputation for being boring and fans can embrace this. All of which is to say, a unique kind of uncertainty is intrinsic to the appeal of sport. This leads to another point.

Rationality imbues an agent with a simplified universal set of characteristics. Sports attendance, however, seems to follow a rationale—a reasoning process informed by contextualising emotions and developed bonds. In the ethnographic section I referred to 'we', meaning several different things: I and my friends and family ('we'), Preston North End fans in general but more specifically the partisan crowd in the stadium ('we'), and the combination of fans and the team, that is 'the club' in its broadest sense ('we'). Attendance is a collective experience in all these senses. It presupposes an 'us' and a 'them' (and there are as many uses of 'them' as 'us'). The decision to attend presupposes participation in these bonds and their meaning to the attendee and this surely extends beyond attendance to the thought process involved in the decision to attend. Anyone who has engaged in this kind of activity will recognise the type of conversations had: 'are *we* going to the match?', 'see *you* at the match', 'where shall *we* meet?', 'don't forget to renew your season ticket', 'there's a season ticket about to become available next to *us*'. You can probably think of variations on these sentences but what they all reveal is that the thought process is not individual and self-regarding. It is communicative. It will either involve imagining what significant others might say, or actual communication and conversation with some of those significant others.

If we refer back to the ethnographic section, the depth of relationships varied enormously, but they all mattered. Wearing replica kit and memorabilia leads to nods of acknowledgement that we support the same team, visiting the same places on the way to the ground leads to nods of recognition and a sense of belonging in otherwise hostile places, sitting in a seat that someone else occupied for years leads to reminiscence regarding their absence, sitting next to others leads to conversations about what they did when they were absent as well as conversation focused on why we are all where we are (the game, the team). Knowledge of how the crowd treat particular players (and particular rival teams) as well as the words to songs and chants leads to knowledgeable participation. All this adds a sense of belonging and thus meaning. It does not require knowing anything more about these others (the 'we', the crowd) for it to be significant. There is affinity. In other cases, the bonds are different, years of conversation with Paul and Chris rarely went beyond football specific themes. My relationship with Michael, of course, is very different since it transcends context, as did (does) Michael's with Paul.

Difference also extends to the nature of payment. Clearly, paying on the day or buying a season ticket is different kinds of acts, but neither presupposes a standard economic agent. The former is more like a spot price and the latter involves paying far in advance. Tickets on the day rarely become cheaper if the team fail to perform during the season and while attendance may reduce this is not necessarily a given. Well-supported teams will still sell out their stadium, irrespective of results (at least up to a point and over a period of time). Season tickets are a different order of commitment in the face of the unique kind of uncertainty intrinsic to the appeal of sport. Teams with little or no chance of success in the 'we will win the league' or 'we will win the cup' sense still attract fans and thus attendance and this includes season ticket holders. Supporters engage in support by definition and fans adapt their goals to what is possible and within the context of perpetual optimism (realistic or otherwise): avoiding relegation, finishing in the top third of the league, qualifying for Europe, etc., and while during the season these may become less likely or impossible, fans still turn up because part of belonging is achieving success together and 'suffering' together.

It is important, however, to emphasise that not everyone will be a 'fan' and that degrees of commitment will be different and there will also be differences between competitive sports (basketball, baseball, American football, football, hockey, rugby league, rugby union, Australian rules football, netball, etc.) and between experience in different countries. Moreover, it would be dangerous to assume that everyone's experience replicates mine (as a fully able white British middle-aged cisgender male).[19] The nature of community and belonging and so on may be different for differently abled, LGBTQ+ and so on potential attendees, so it would be inappropriate to substitute a single alternative for the standard economic

---

[19] Note: there is a great deal of research on this kind of issues in sociology and cultural studies. See, for example Cleland and Cashmore (2016).

agent. That, however, is not what I am trying to achieve. The existence of variation implies that not only community but heterogeneity matters, but it remains the case that no version of the experience associated with attendance or whether to attend seems to resemble the standard economic agent. Using it as a starting point seems a wholly inappropriate way to understand and explain what is going on in team sports attendance.

While the issues I've raised receive little attention within sports economics, for reasons I have previously discussed and which I have summarised in the introduction (hence the need for debate), it stretches credibility to think that sports economists are unaware of the limitations imposed by adopting the standard economic agent from mainstream microeconomics. Some outside the core of the field have indicated a degree of concern—motivated, for example, by sociology or psychology (e.g. James, 2001; Koo & Hardin, 2008; Kim et al., 2019) or by an interaction with nonmainstream economics (e.g. Lera-López et al., 2011; Lera-López et al., 2012), but this has not translated into an alternative.[20] The main strategy has been to identify variables of concern, loosen assumptions and discuss behavioural bias or consider limitations of method. It might, however, also be argued that the lack of discussion of an alternative approach to the economic agent for sports attendance demand is because sports economics has found itself on the wrong side of a general dividing line in economics.[21] I now turn briefly to this.

---

[20] Despite the involvement of prominent heterodox economists such as Paul Downward.

[21] Note, there can be considerable variation and nuance within the dominant side of the divide. For example, the *Handbook of Sports Economics Research* decomposes research into sports microeconomics and sportometrics, both of which deal with the dominant side. Consider: 'I define a sports economist as one who does research on sports-related topics. There are two unique, but not mutually exclusive, strains of sports related research. First, in order of appearance in the literature, there is a research that applies microeconomic theory to the sports industry in an attempt to understand the market of sports. This strain can be referred to as "sports microeconomics" and contains papers that develop or adapt economic theory for use in describing the sports industry. The history of such studies spans some 50 years. In the past 30 years, another literature has developed that uses sports data to test or explain various components of microeconomic theory. Goff and Tollinson (2010) call this type of research "sportometrics" comparing it to experimental economics that uses data from sporting contests instead of laboratory data. The intent of these two strains differ; sports microeconomics has a narrowing focus, from the larger field of microeconomics to the smaller field of sports economics, while sportometrics has an expanding focus, from sports economics to microeconomics. Although there is clearly room for both in sports economics, the "sportometrician" is more concerned with acceptance outside the subdiscipline than is the sports microeconomist. It is incumbent on sports economists to explain their research can be generalized beyond the sports industry, something which they have become increasingly adept' (Jewell, 2017, p. 9).

Three Versions of a Dividing Line

There are at least three ways to discuss the existence of a dividing line in economics, which seem relevant to our discussion. First, the well-known economic sociologist Mark Granovetter, observes that there are two contrasting views of the sociality of economic interaction: first, the under-socialised view taken by neoclassical economics, and second, an over-socialised view taken by others (Granovetter, 1985, 2017). Interestingly, he finds neither satisfactory, since neither allows agency to make a real difference—instead, theory shifts from an individual conforming to a limited sense of calculative self-interest to one that has internalised external sources of compulsion. While Granovetter provides a good example of a theorist who takes seriously the need for both social structure and agency in economic decision-making, the main reason to draw attention to his work here is that it highlights two perspectives on sociality that affect theory.

The political economist William K. Tabb provides a second interesting way to highlight dividing lines. In his book *Reconstructing Political Economy: The great divide in economic thought* Tabb argues that economics has split into two cultures, an A category and a B category. He appropriates the concept of 'two cultures' from CP Snow. For Tabb, economics can be divided into:

> A social *science* economists and B *social* science economists. The A group takes physics as its model. Not modern physics, with its interest in chaos and complexity, but seventeenth-, eighteenth- and nineteenth-century physics, bolstered by a theorem-driven mathematical fundamentalism. B science (which ironically is more like modern physics than is A type economic science) is historical, institutional, and comparative. Contingency and agency are important for B type economists. The hard-core A practitioners can be condescending to B economists, hoping they someday will learn to use deterministic mathematical models and test their theories by making predictions that they then verify statistically and so come to understand economic laws. B mode thinkers can think the As narrow and simple minded. (Tabb, 1999, pp. 18–19)

Tabb provides a useful way to reflect on the role power plays in economics. The A social *science* economists have most of the prestige and dominate education and resources and because of this economics has tended to deal poorly with sociality.

Tabb, however, is not the only person to observe that economics main dividing line is focused on what kind of science economics aspires to be (and also whether it should aspire to be a science at all). For example, Philip Mirowski's *More Heat than Light: Economics as Social Physics, Physics as Nature's Economics* makes a similar point (Mirowski, 1989) as does, from the reverse side of the case, the well-known original institutionalist economist Geoff Hodgson in *How Economics Forgot History* (Hodgson, 2001). Whatever differences there might be in the specific arguments of Tabb, Mirowski and Hodgson each thinks that economics has also split along methodological grounds and this brings me to a third way to describe a dividing line in economics which draws its concepts from philosophy of social science.

According to the realist critique in economics, which has since the 1990s centred on Cambridge, the main dividing line in economics is between theory and methods that presuppose a 'closed system' and those that work with 'open systems'. Based on this distinction the preference for mathematical modelling has led to an inappropriate approach to economic phenomena, since the successful application of these mathematical models depend on the existence of closed systems and closed systems are rare. Closed systems have highly regular operation and outcomes.[22] Given this, the assumptions used in economic theory and methods and the outcomes sought are a mismatch to how things are. Because social reality is an open

[22] According to Lawson there are two conditions necessary for closure, each with several aspects. First, the intrinsic closure condition, which 'entails two essential aspects'. 'A first constraint ... is that of *intrinsic constancy*: that the internal, or intrinsic structure of any (delineated state of any) individual of analysis be constant. The second obvious requirement (of any theoretical construction that is to satisfy the intrinsic condition for a closure) is *reducibility*: that the overall outcome event, for any state description, be reducible to the system conditions obtaining. Clearly the conditions of intrinsic constancy and reducibility are both automatically satisfied if any and every relevant individual is characterised atomistically' (Lawson, 1997, p. 98). The second closure condition is 'extrinsic closure' and this simply means that nothing outside of the stated conditions has an effect (Lawson, 1997, p. 99). So, intrinsic closure refers to clearly defined isolated relationships between variables in the form of regularities, and extrinsic closure means that nothing beyond these isolated regular relationships are relevant. Note, the post-Keynesians Victoria Chick and Sheila Dow have a slightly different concept of open systems (Chick & Dow, 2005).

system regularity is partial, contingent, localised and tends eventually to break down. From this point of view, theory and methods should be adapted to how the world actually is and focus on identifying underlying but shifting causal mechanisms. Tony Lawson is perhaps the best-known proponent of this point of view (Lawson, 1997, 2003, 2015a, 2015b).[23]

In any case, for our purposes it seems clear that sports economics has opted for an approach that under-socialises the agent, adopts an A category social *science* perspective and presupposes closed systems. The final thing I want to achieve in this chapter is an illustration of the potential offered to economists by the other side of the divide for an alternative approach to sports attendance. The other side explores economics as social theory. Its theorists are acutely aware that this involves some version of what is typically referred to as the 'agent-structure problem' (something we briefly mentioned above). Interested theorists explore a range of overlapping concepts including culture, institutions, habit, rules, roles and positions (among others) as possible ways to explain how real agents act and why.

A Few Illustrations of the Potential of the Other Side of the Divide

In philosophy, social theory and methodology 'ontology' refer to theory of being. The concept of ontology is easily misunderstood. It does not mean 'x is definitely how reality is' and therefore 'x is true'. Like any theory, ontology can be found to apply only in some times and places, it can be only partially insightful in its claims, or can turn out to be wrong. The main attraction of the concept is that it forces us to ask, 'what do our theories and methods explicitly or implicitly assume reality to be like and is this consistent with what we observe around us or with what we think we know?' The concept of agency that has been dominant in the economics of sports attendance demand involves an obvious ontological mismatch. The agents we see (and some of us are) are not like the agents found in typical theory and models. There are, however, economists and social

---

[23] Lawson argues in addition that non-mainstream economics is not just united by its opposition to mainstream economics but also by its advocacy of open systems. However, since 'heterodox' economists must also pursue careers in existing economics departments and publish according to the expectations of journals, there is a fundamental tension and a tendency to still adopt inappropriate methods. See Lawson (2015a, 2015b, Chap. 3).

theorists who work with a different more contextualised and social concept of agency. What follows is a brief selection and is not intended to be comprehensive. Each highlights a slightly different concept relevant for how we understand agency.[24]

One of the main problematic features of the standard economic agent is that they make decisions in isolation and as an individual. Geoff Hodgson, who I have already mentioned, states:

> The social world, by virtue of the fact that it is social, must involve interactive relations … society consists not merely of individuals, but also of interactions between individuals, plus interactions between individuals and other aspects of their environment including, presumably, both the natural world and other socio-economic systems. (Hodgson, 2007, pp. 3–4)[25]

Geoff Hodgson is a proponent of original institutional economics (OIE). As the name suggests, OIE places great emphasis on the development of institutions, defined 'as systems of established and prevalent social rules that structure social interactions. Language, money, law, systems of weights and measures, table manners and firms (and other organizations) are thus all institutions' (Hodgson, 2006, p. 2). These institutions affect who agents are in a situation, and how agents both think and act. Arguably, sport is institutional.

Moving on, Edward Fullbrook, editor of *Real-World Economics Review*, places great emphasis on what interdependency suggests about the context and meaning of agency. He states that 'interdependencies between the tastes, preferences, demands, goals, ethics, perceptions and decisions of economic actors are pervasive' (Fullbrook, 2002a, 2002b, p. i). He distinguishes intersubjective and intra-subjective concepts of agency:

> A purely intra-subjective interaction between two human subjects or between a human subject and socio-cultural economic structures (for

---

[24] Note: I am not implying that the concepts are mutually exclusive or solely associated with the theorists I discuss.

[25] Note: Hodgson includes the following footnote: 'The term "social" here is used in a broad sense, to encompass phenomena that are examined in economics, as well as other social sciences. In the social context all relations between individuals are causal and interactive, at least in the sense that in maintaining these relations with others, individuals are affected by their (partial) awareness of them and different actions may be enabled. Accordingly, the term "interactive relations" in the social context can be replaced by just "relations"' (Hodgson, 2007, footnote 7).

example, markets), is one that leaves the subjects, like Newton's atoms, unchanged as entities. In intersubjective interaction is one that does not. [... A more realistic approach to agency has two tasks] First, concepts of non-atomistic agents must be formed, concepts subtle enough to capture the ambiguity and complexity of the intersubjective agent. Second, social, cultural and economic structures created by such agents must be identified and analysed in terms of the way they in turn shape and reshape the agents. (Fullbrook, 2002a, 2002b, pp. 2–3)[26]

Sport attendance is very obviously a context which shapes and reshapes the agent. The quote from Fullbrook is taken from the introduction to his edited collection *Intersubjectivity in Economics: Agents and Structures*. The collection contains essays by well-known academics from the French 'economics of conventions' school, original institutionalism and social economics. Among the contributors are Hodgson and John B. Davis. Davis's work is also worth comment.

Davis has done a lot of work on the concept of care in economics but also on identity. In his book *The Theory of the Individual in Economics: Identity and Value* he makes the point that:

beginning to think systematically about individuals as endogenous to the economic process depends upon first developing a framework for discussing individuality and the nature of individuals. (Davis, 2003, p. 11)[27]

---

[26] Note: Fullbrook argues that the neoclassical atomistic individual agent was not always wholly inappropriate and intra-subjective situations have existed.

[27] For Davis, economics has been overly focused on a narrow theory of choice which makes it impossible to make sense of the complexity of real individuals. He refers to the theory as subjectivist, meaning subjective theory of value associated with marginalism since the 1800s. The book discusses a long history of the concept of the individual and argues this has its origins in modernist 'dualism' (outer objective world and inner subjective mind). He makes a similar point to Fullbrook regarding intra-subjectivity. In economics the identity of the agent is unchanged from time T1 to T2 and economics deals poorly with the 'reidentification problem'. He also suggests there is an 'individuation problem': 'How, then, are we to know when individuals ought to be subsumed within groups of individuals and when they ought to be regarded as distinct agents?' (Davis, 2003, p. 13). Davis is clear that 'neoclassical and mainstream economics, which make the individual central to their analysis, lack an adequate conception of the individual' and 'heterodox economics, which does not generally emphasize the individual, in fact offers elements of an adequate theory of the individual' (Davis, 2003, p. 17).

Davis explores different ways the individual has been conceptualised in relation to identity. Personal identity has often presupposed a coherent self-contained individual whose identity is unchanged by interaction or context. For Davis, however, neither of these is true (i.e. unchanged by interaction or context) and we need a better understanding of personal identity that is more consistent with diverse social contexts and with the possibility of change through interaction. For Davis, we do not become fractured or lacking in identity because we are social. We are adaptable and changing. Davis is clear that an individual is 'embedded' and any adequate concept of the agent should pay attention to the specifics of how they are embedded. A universal concept of agency focused on calculation can tell one little about this.

Mary Wrenn is another whose work might provide a useful alternative way of thinking from the other side of the divide in economics. Wrenn is another well-known institutionalist (and former Joan Robinson research fellow at Girton College Cambridge). In her article 'Agency and mental models in heterodox economics' she begins from a reference to Davis's 2003 work but makes the point that agency must be 'examined' according to 'how it came to be and how it evolves' (Wrenn, 2006, p. 483; also 2018, p. 177). According to Wrenn, drawing among others on Davis and Hodgson, as agents we each have 'mental models' and this is a key feature of how we engage with the diversity of the world:

> Instinct, habit, and patterns of behaviour form the building blocks of the individual's mental models. The individual is born with certain instincts that have evolved since the emergence of man, such as the capacity for language. Humans must have an innate sense of how to communicate in order to physically manipulate the body to produce sound. Once a human is able to communicate, interaction with the surrounding structural context, including intersubjective relationships with other individuals, builds up the range of language, including dialect and culturally specific rhetoric. Habits and instincts are part of the cognitive framework, in other words, part of an individual's mental models, and are at least partially informed by institutions and structure. Habits, routines, competency base, and skills are not static but evolve with the changing structure and the changing individual ... Habituation is a stabilizing and creative force in terms of institutional formation and evolution, as well as stabilized and channelled by the surrounding structural context... As such, institutions and individuals maintain their independence while simultaneously are interdependent. (Wrenn, 2006, p. 484)

Wrenn argues that agency is influenced by the situations we find ourselves in and the choices we make over a lifetime—the many life experiences we have. The sociality of sports attendance can relatively easily be translated into these terms. Attendance is habituated and cultural. It has its specific rituals and roles that individuals either fall into or choose.[28]

Attendance at a sports event requires one to choose to take part and this has a significance that is more than transactional. There is more to 'intention' than individual calculation and I bring this section to a close with a brief reference to the work of the Stanford philosopher Michael Bratman. There are many philosophers and social theorists who are well-known for their work on the agent-structure problem (e.g. John Searle, Anthony Giddens and Margaret Archer), but Bratman is especially interesting because of his work on 'shared agency' and 'collective intentionality' (see Bratman, 1999, 2007, 2014). For Bratman, shared intention fulfils three tasks: coordinating actions, coordinating planning and structuring bargaining. His focus for some of this is everyday activity between individuals which does not depend on formal institutional structures. It is informal togetherness. I would suggest the decision to attend a sports event seems very obviously of this kind.

To summarise, concepts of institutions, intersubjectivity, identity formation, mental models and shared agency are all possible ways to conceptualise the economic agent differently than is currently the case. To put this slightly differently, each seems more in line with the 'social ontology' of a real agent.

Conclusion

In this chapter I have made four main points. First, sports attendance is a highly social and collective experience. Second, while there has been some progress in developing a concept of the agent, this has mainly focused on introducing new variables of interest and datasets and on identifying 'bias'. There has been little or no discussion of the adequacy of the agent—hence the need for debate. Third, the economic agent used or presupposed in sports economics still lacks many of the characteristics a real attendee might exhibit. Fourth, given the sociality of sports attendance, this seems to put sports economics on the wrong side of a more general divide in

---

[28] Note: this is consistent with an emergent and stratified social ontology. In general, all the theorists share an open systems approach to social reality and this includes the concepts of emergence. Emergence is a concept that reality has aspects whose powers are made possible by the organisation of parts and which cannot be reduced to those parts in isolation. See, for example Davis (2016, p. 142).

economics. Following these four points I have also provided a brief illustration of concepts of social agency from the other side of the divide.

As a final point there may be a temptation to dismiss some of the argument I have made on the basis that the evidence I provide regarding the social agent is anecdotal or personal. I would, however, note that the argument mainly turns on the critique of the plausibility of the construction and assumptions of the standard economic agent and its contrast to experiences that many will recognise. Moreover, there is in fact a great deal of peripheral acknowledgement that there are problems with the standard construction, but researchers have adopted a typical strategy found in economics, which is to acknowledge that a model may be a simplification and involve some aspects whose realism can be questioned. This amounts to 'carrying on regardless'.[29]

The next task is to develop an alternative more social approach to attendance demand in sports economics. One useful way forward is to combine work on embedded agency with lesser-known potentials from behavioural economics. Daniel Kahneman is best known for his work with Amos Tversky on Prospect Theory. However, Kahneman also developed work on agency that is very different to this. Rather than a theory of agency which only applies in 'closed systems', a combination of embedded agency and Kahneman's agent can result in a social ontology of agency which is consistent with an 'open systems' approach.[30]

---

[29] For example, Downward et al. (2009) recognise that there is a 'methodological conundrum in economics' in relation to reality. The relaxing of assumptions can lead to the model being inappropriately applied. In other papers, researchers have acknowledged the limitations of their model specification—often suggesting significant weaknesses or philosophical inconsistencies, but have applied the model anyway, such as Lera-Lopez et al. (2011).

[30] Note: behavioural economics has been classified as one of the schools of thought that extends mainstream sports economics in terms of psychological foundations (see Thomas & Tierney, 2021). Much, however, depends on what we mean by behavioural economics. In his cognitive psychology work in the 1970s, Kahneman took an interest in group dynamics, and use of dynamic 'feedback' from other's behaviour in our actions and preferences, but this was not fully developed in his work with Tversky. For example, in most of the major professional sports events (e.g. football, rugby, cricket) the contest is set between two teams of competitors and the fans tend to be divided into two partisan groups, each of whom offer support to one team or the other. The (often) contrary emotions felt and demonstrated by fans create an environment of anticipation, expectation, enjoyment, excitement and nervousness—and organically fosters very powerful social bonds amongst groups, and often conflict between opposing groups. The organic noise and intensity of social interaction at sports events are what influences many spectators to make their attendance decision. The emotional rollercoaster of fan's support—for all the participants—is contagious and is impossible to simulate. This is most certainly not an atomistic form of consumption.

REFERENCES

Andreff, W. (2022). Oldies but Goldies! Twenty years after, the journal of sports economics at a crossroads? *Journal of Sports Economics, 23*(6), 659–727.

Atkinson, M. (2016). Ethnography. In B. Smith & A. C. Sparkes (Eds.), *(2019). Routledge handbook of qualitative research in sports and exercise* (pp. 49–61). Routledge.

Bizzozero, P., Flepp, R., & Franck, E. (2016). The importance of suspense and surprise in entertainment demand: Evidence from Wimbledon. *Journal of Economic Behavior & Organization, 130*, 47–63.

Black, R. D. C. (2017). Utility. In M. Vernengo, E. Caldentey, & B. Rosser Jr. (Eds.), *The new Palgrave dictionary of economics*. Palgrave Macmillan. Online continuously updating version.

Borland, J., & MacDonald, R. (2003). Demand for sport. *Oxford Review of Economic Policy, 19*(1), 478–502.

Bratman, M. E. (1999). *Intention, plans and practical reason*. Harvard University Press.

Bratman, M. E. (2007). *Structures of agency: Essays*. Oxford University Press.

Bratman, M. E. (2014). *Shared agency: A planning theory of acting together*. Oxford University Press.

Chalmers, A. (2019). Atomism from the 17th to the 20th century. *The Stanford Encyclopedia of Philosophy*, (Spring 2019 Edition), Edward N. Zalta (ed.). https://plato.stanford.edu/archives/spr2019/entries/atomism-modern/

Chick, V., & Dow, S. (2005). The meaning of open systems. *Journal of Economic Methodology, 12*(3), 363–381.

Cleland, J., & Cashmore, E. (2016). Football fans' view of racism in British football. *International Review for the Sociology of Sport, 51*(1), 27–43.

Davis, J. B. (2003). *The theory of the individual in economics: Identity and value*. Routledge.

Davis, J. B. (2016). Lawson on Veblen on social ontology. In J. Morgan (Ed.), *What is neoclassical economics?* (pp. 135–148). Routledge.

Dow, S. (2012). The non-neutrality of formalism. In S. Dow (Ed.), *Foundations for new economic thinking* (pp. 140–161). Macmillan.

Downward, P., Dawson, A., & Dejonghe, E. (2009). *Sports economics: Theory, evidence and policy*. Routledge.

Fourcade, M., Ollion, E., & Algan, Y. (2015). The superiority of economists. *Journal of Economic Perspectives, 29*(1), 89–114.

Fullbrook, E. (2002a). Why intersubjectivity? In E. Fullbrook (Ed.), *Intersubjectivity in economics—Agents and structures* (pp. 1–10). Routledge.

Fullbrook, E. (Ed.). (2002b). *Intersubjectivity in economics*. Routledge.

Granovetter, M. (1985). Economic action and social structure: The problem of embeddedness. *American Journal of Sociology, 91*(3), 481–510.

Granovetter, M. (2017). *Society and economy: Framework and principles.* Belknap Press.

Grix, J., Brannagan, P. M., Grimes, H., & Neville, R. (2021). The impact of Covid-19 on sport. *International Journal of Sport Policy and Politics, 13*(1), 1–12.

Hall, J., O'Mahony, B., & Vieceli, J. (2010). An empirical model of attendance factors at major sporting events. *International Journal of Hospitality Management, 29*(2), 328–334.

Hamilton, D. (2018). *Going to the match: The passion for football.* Hodder and Stoughton.

Hargreaves-Heap, S., & Clark, C. (2017). Economic man. In M. Vernengo, E. Caldentey, & B. Rosser Jr. (Eds.), *The new Palgrave dictionary of economics.* Palgrave Macmillan. Online continuously updating version.

Hodgson, G. (2001). *How economics forgot history: The problem of historical specificity in social science.* Routledge.

Hodgson, G. (2006). What are institutions? *Journal of Economic Issues, 40*(1), 1–25.

Hodgson, G. (2007). Meanings of methodological individualism. *Journal of Economic Methodology, 14*(2), 211–226.

James, J. (2001). The role of cognitive development and socialization in the initial development of team loyalty. *Leisure Sciences, 23*(4), 233–261.

Jewell, R. T. (2017). Sports economics: The state of the discipline. In J. Fizel (Ed.), *Handbook of sports economic research* (pp. 9–18). Routledge.

Johnson, C. (2021). Loss aversion, reference-dependent preferences, and collective bargaining agreements in the National Basketball Association. *International Journal of Sport Finance, 16*(2), 69–78.

Kim, Y., Magnusen, M., Kim, M., & Lee, H. (2019). Meta-analytic review of sport consumption: Factors affecting attendance to sporting event. *Sport Marketing Quarterly, 28*(3), 117–134.

Klamer, A., & Colander, D. (1990). *The making of an economist.* Westview Press.

Koo, G. Y., & Hardin, R. (2008). Difference in interrelationship between spectators' motives and behavioral intentions based on emotional attachment. *Sport Marketing Quarterly, 17*(1), 30–43.

Lawson, T. (1997). *Economics and reality.* Routledge.

Lawson, T. (2003). *Reorienting economics.* Routledge.

Lawson, T. (2015a). *Essays on the nature and state of modern economics.* Routledge.

Lawson, T. (2015b). *The nature and state of modern economics.* Routledge.

Lera-López, F., Ollo-López, A., & Rapún-Gárate, M. (2012). Sports spectatorship in Spain: Attendance and consumption. *European Sport Management Quarterly, 12*(3), 265–289.

Lera-López, F., Rapún-Gárate, M., & Suárez, M. J. (2011). Determinants of individual consumption on sports attendance in Spain. *International Journal of Sport Finance, 6*(3), 204–221.

Machina, M. J. (2008). Expected utility hypothesis. In S. N. Durlauf & L. E. Blume (Eds.), *The new Palgrave dictionary of economics* (2nd ed.). Palgrave Macmillan.

Mearman, A., Berger, S., & Guizzo, D. (2018). Is UK economics teaching changing? Evaluating the new subject benchmark statement. *Review of Social Economy, 76*(3), 377–396.

Meir, R., & Scott, D. (2007). Tribalism: Definition, identification and relevance to the marketing of professional sports franchises. *International Journal of Sports Marketing and Sponsorship, 8*(4), 43–59.

Mirowski, P. (1989). *More heat than light: Economics as social physics, physics as Nature's economics.* Cambridge University Press.

Neale, W. C. (1964). The peculiar economics of professional sports: A contribution to the theory of the firm in sporting competition and in market competition. *The Quarterly Journal of Economics, 78*(1), 1–14.

Proops, I. (2022). Wittgenstein's logical atomism. *The Stanford encyclopedia of philosophy* (Fall 2022 Edition), Edward N. Zalta and Uri Nodelman (Eds.). https://plato.stanford.edu/archives/fall2022/entries/wittgenstein-atomism/

Rewilak, J. (2023). The designated player policy rule and attendance demand in Major League Soccer. *Journal of Sports Economics, 24*(4), 475–496.

Richardson, T., Nalbantis, G., & Pawlowski, T. (2023). Emotional cues and the demand for televised sports: Evidence from the UEFA champions league. *Journal of Sports Economics, 24*(8), 993–1025.

Rosenthal, T. G. (2009). *L.S. Lowry—The art and the artist.* Unicorn press.

Rottenberg, S. (1956). The baseball players labor market. *Journal of Political Economy, 64*(3), 242–258.

Shafer, W. (2017). Transitivity. In M. Vernengo, E. Caldentey, & B. Rosser Jr. (Eds.), *The new Palgrave dictionary of economics.* Palgrave Macmillan. Online continuously updating version.

Skrok, L. (2016). The pitfalls of econometric tests of the uncertainty of outcome hypothesis: Interdependence of variables, imperfect proxies, and unstable parabols. *International Journal of Sport Finance, 11*(3), 232–246.

Sloane, P. J. (1971). The economics of professional football: The football club as utility maximiser. *Scottish Journal of Political Economy, 18*(2), 121–146.

Statista. (2022). Professional sports overview. Last viewed 1st October 2023. https://www.statista.com/markets/409/topic/627/professional-sports/#overview

Sung, H., & Pyun, H. (2023). Disaggregated attendance demand: Comparing daily ticket purchasers and season ticket holders in K-league 1. *Journal of Sports Economics, 24*(6), 717–736.

Tabb, W. (1999). *Reconstructing political economy: The great divide in economic thought.* Routledge.

Thomas, S., & Tierney, K. (2021). Institutional dynamics in Sport. In H. J. R. Altman, M. Altman, & B. Torgler (Eds.), *Behavioural sports economics: A research companion* (pp. 78–96). Routledge.

Wrenn, M. V. (2006). Agency and mental models in heterodox economics. *Journal of Economics Issues, 40*(2), 483–491.

Wrenn, M. V. (2018). Heterodox economics and theories of interactive agency. In T. H. Jo, L. Chester, & C. D'ippolita (Eds.), *The Routledge handbook of heterodox economics: Theorizing, analyzing and transforming capitalism* (pp. 176–187). Routledge.

CHAPTER 4

A Critical Realist-Behavioural Economics Hybrid Theory of Sports Attendance Demand: The View from the Other Side of the Dividing Line in Economics

Abstract This chapter begins from the question, 'if we *don't* start from the standard economic agent, what does a theory of and research strategy for sports attendance demand look like?' In order to develop an answer to this question over a series of sections, I first 'go back to basics' on the understanding that there is a divide in economics and much of sports attendance demand research is on one side of that divide. In a series of sections, I develop a set of concepts drawing on critical realism, in order to eventually place attendance demand within an open systems non-atomistic agent-structure framework. I then turn to behavioural economics and make the case that Daniel Kahneman's work can be resituated within this approach. Finally, I discuss a research strategy consistent with the framework developed.

Keywords Sports economics • Attendance demand • Critical realism • Kahneman

J. Embery, *Attendance Demand in Sports Economics*, Palgrave Pivots in Sports Economics,
https://doi.org/10.1007/978-3-031-60040-1_4

INTRODUCTION

Based on an extensive survey of the field, I have previously argued that sports economics uses or presupposes an economic agent that is drawn originally from neoclassical economics.[1] While there has been some development and modification of the concept of the agent in sports economics, a standard economic agent remains the benchmark. This agent makes isolated and calculative decisions. Methodologists refer to this isolation as atomism. I have previously argued that this warrants debate and reconsideration, since atomism is especially problematic for sports attendance because attendance is a quintessentially social activity. Arguably, this has placed much of the work on attendance demand on the wrong side of a more general dividing line in economics.

On one side of the divide are economists who prefer a precise specification of an agent's actions and decision-making scope. This has tended to assume away (at least to begin with) much of what we know is important to an agent attending a sports event, especially a fan. It leads to a heavy emphasis on models which allow measurable tests of the strength of relations of variables of interest, but at the expense of adequate representation of the deep sense of enduring attachment, emotion, partisanship and community which inform attendance. The 'mainstream' or dominant way of doing economics stands on this side of the divide and so it is entirely explicable that sports economics, insofar as it aspires to be 'economics', typically finds itself on this side of the divide. On the other side of the divide, however, are economists who work with the diverse contexts, motivations, practices and reasoning of agents—the sociality of the experience and its consequences for decision-making. In this chapter I intend to sketch a theory of sports attendance demand and research strategy appropriate to this other side of the divide. Following my previous work on this subject, the question I pose takes it as given that there is a problem with the use of the standard economic agent in sports attendance demand and asks, 'if we *don't* start from the standard economic agent, what does a theory of and research strategy for sports attendance demand look like?'

Since the question asked is a fundamental one, which implicitly looks to place sports economics on the other side of a divide heavily weighted to the opposing side of that divide, it makes sense to first go back to basics. I

---

[1] Note: throughout the chapter I switch between use of 'I' and 'we' as appropriate to context.

have previously introduced the concept of ontology. Ontology is 'theory of being' and its main attraction is that it allows us to ask, 'what do our theories and methods explicitly or implicitly assume reality to be like and is this consistent with what we observe around us or with what we think we know?' While this type of question is drawn from philosophy, it is not unheard of in economics. Joseph Schumpeter, for example, early in his *History of Economic Analysis* observes that what we consider appropriate to the construction of theory and methods is influenced by a 'pre-analytic' vision that frames our thinking (Schumpeter, 1997/1954, p. 42).

I start from an initial focus on ontology since it allows us to develop a series of concepts and insights to address the mismatch between the agent we observe in sports attendance and the agent we assume for theory and modelling purposes. In principle, this should facilitate a more consistent approach, where our theory and use of methods is not at odds with the phenomena under investigation. I have also previously introduced the distinction between a closed and an open system. A closed system refers to a set of relationships or an entity (such as an agent) or collection of entities whose mode of action is self-contained and highly regular in its outcomes (it has specified conditions which facilitate 'event regularity'). An open system in contrast is neither entirely self-contained nor highly regular.[2]

A focus on ontology allows us to usefully place the closed and open system distinction within a broader set of concepts, which in turn allows us to reconsider sports attendance demand as an agent-structure social-economic theory problem. There are various approaches to ontology

---

[2] Note: as I have previously acknowledged, there are different takes on the nature of open and closed systems. This account is drawn from critical realism and the early work of Tony Lawson and Roy Bhaskar. It focuses on the role of event regularity. Others, such as Victoria Chick and Sheila Dow, argue that this can be misleading. A closed system can be highly complex and chaotic in its operation and in reality no system is fully closed and all are open to some degree. Arguably, the different points of view expressed in this debate are working at cross purposes and using slightly different definitions. Closed system is a heuristic device to expose a general problem of atomism. All agree that isolated atomistic event regularity is a problematic way to conceptualise social phenomena and that mainstream economics suffers from this problem. All agree that there are degrees of stability or regularity in outcomes for phenomena that can at any moment become irregular and a better way forward is to work with a more diverse and complex concept of social action. See later references and discussion.

available from philosophy, social theory and methodology.[3] I use a version of 'critical realism'. This is for three main reasons. First, the main claims are well-developed, coherent and highly relevant to the issues we have raised. Second, critical realism has been extensively discussed and developed in the context of economic discourse by 'heterodox' economists.[4] Third, while there is significant debate regarding the use of methods consistent with claims on ontology, which has also led to debate among interested economists on whether critical realism is an approach they are prepared to adopt, realism (as I shall make clear) has concepts and makes claims which seek to make sense of and work with differences (see also Morgan & Embery, 2018).

Similar to ontology, there are a variety of available treatments of the agent-structure problem that all seek to achieve the same thing: provide context which shapes what an agent thinks is appropriate and what they can do, but which does not preclude scope for the agent to reflect on their situation, make genuine choices and work to change the conditions in which choices are made. Social theory drawing on critical realism offers several variations on what Roy Bhaskar refers to as the 'transformational model of social activity' (TMSA). Since my focus is mainly on the role of the agent I opt to combine this with a version of agency drawn from behavioural economics. This has at least two other attractions. First, it can reasonably be assumed that most sports economists are familiar with behavioural economics and what it sets out to achieve. Second, there is a version of behavioural economics that can be synthesised from Daniel Kahneman's work in particular that seems suited to the side of the divide in economics I am concerned with. Working with this version allows us to begin to develop a research strategy that offers a critical realist-behavioural economics hybrid for sports attendance demand.

With the above in mind in a first series of short sections I introduce critical realism and provide simple explanations of key concepts that any

---

[3] Note: the terminology for this varies. Research methods textbooks often introduce a simple set of categories that are supposed to structure approaches to methods, especially the divide between quantitative and qualitative methods. The typical range set out includes positivism, realism and social constructivism. See, for example Bell et al. (2022, pp. 20–38). This covers the standard categories of research approaches. However, this can be misleading. Not only does each have a history, many internal debates and a great deal of diversity, but also each is essentially a set of claims about reality. See my later discussion of research methods.

[4] Well-known edited collections focused on realism in economics include Fleetwood (1999), Lewis (2004), Fullbrook (2009) and Pratten (2015).

interested general reader might follow. I then provide a transition section which highlights why this initial material is relevant to theory and research on sports attendance demand. I then turn to behavioural economics in a further series of sections. Drawing on Kahneman's work with Amos Tversky, I set out the common approach taken to behavioural economics and then set out material which illustrates that there is more diversity and development in the field than this might imply. This provides scope to consider a 'path not taken' and I then turn to Kahneman's evolving attitude to his work and some of the developments that can be identified in his later work, especially *Thinking Fast and Slow*. Based on the argument made I suggest Kahneman's work can be placed on the other side of the divide in economics. Finally, I turn to two sections which set out a possible way forward which combine the previous work (hence hybrid). I set out a research strategy and highlight an approach to use of methods. I would emphasise that the chapter is constrained by what can reasonably be discussed and developed in a few thousand words. To reiterate, the following is a 'sketch' and the intention is to make the case for a 'strategy'. The argument does not turn on detailed empirical application or data and I do no more than highlight potentials.

An Introduction to Critical Realism

Critical realism emerged in the 1970s as an original position within debates in philosophy of science and developed through the 1980s and 1990s as a philosophy of social science. The International Association for Critical Realism (IACR) was established in 1997 and the *Journal of Critical Realism* began publication in 2002 (though this was preceded by a previous format titled *Alethia* in 1998). For some, critical realism is closely associated with the work of Roy Bhaskar, but while he is responsible for the earliest formative philosophical texts, there have been many other innovative contributors over the years, of which possibly the best known are Margaret Archer, Bob Jessop, Tony Lawson, Andrew Sayer and most recently Dave Elder-Vass. Bhaskar's later work on 'dialectics' and then 'transcendental dialectical critical realism' resulted in developments that not all critical realists found acceptable and today there are several strands of critical realism. However, there are also underlying concepts and commitments that most, if not all, share and Hubert Buch-Hansen and Peter Nielsen refer to these as 'the basics' (Buch-Hansen & Nielsen, 2020).

Discussion of these is sufficient for our purpose (see also Collier, 1994).[5] You may at first be wondering what the point of some of the following is, but it will become clearer later.

Critical realism starts from the uncontroversial claim that there is no unmediated knowledge of the world and that all substantive theory and use of methods presupposes something about the world (even if the intention is to discover things about the world, one has to make assumptions about what kinds of things there are to discover, understand or explain). Critical realism then sets out to make sense of this by introducing three main concepts and these are ontological realism, epistemological relativism and judgemental rationality. In introducing these I also introduce a series of related and supporting concepts (signalled in the subheadings).

ONTOLOGICAL REALISM, STRATIFICATION, EMERGENCE AND CAUSAL MECHANISM

Ontological realism is the claim that there is a mind-independent reality. The universe pre-exists humans, and while humans can have impacts on the rest of reality, they do so in accordance with what is possible based on the ways of working of existing phenomena. For example, production of plastics depends on the combinatory possibilities of elements to form molecules with given features—these are manipulated to produce plastics. The nature of those molecules in turn affects what happens when they become waste introduced into the environment. However, as this example also hints (since it has producers), while the universe may pre-exist us as a species, society does not. This statement, however, requires careful unpacking.

Critical realists emphasise that while society cannot pre-exist us as a species, it does pre-exist the individual who is born into it and what happens in society does not reduce merely to what an individual thinks. This is important because it means that social reality is a special case of mind-independence. If there were no conscious, self-aware and reflexive beings (us), then there would be no society, so society depends for its existence on the combined activity of people—and not just the living, the accumulated ways of doing things that those in the past bequeath to the present

---

[5] Note: a version of what follows can be found in many other sources that begin by introducing key concepts and developments in critical realism. For example, the edited collection *Critical Realism: Essential Readings* starts from a chapter titled 'Introduction: Basic texts and developments' (Bhaskar & Lawson, 1998). See also the first three chapters of *Economics and Reality* (Lawson, 1997) and the summary chapter on critical realism in Fred Lee and Bruce Cronin's *Handbook of Research Methods and Applications in Heterodox Economics* (Morgan, 2016a, 2016b).

also matter. I cannot make leaves into money just by deciding in my own head that the oak tree in my back garden is an ATM and its leaves are £10 notes. At the same time, if people did not carry in their heads some basic concept of money and payments, then money could not 'exist' and society would be different. This implies that social reality is structured, individually mind-independent in some ways but also mind responsive—what we think and then crucially *do,* based on what we think, matters to how things are and how they happen. This becomes the 'agent-structure problem', which I mentioned in the introduction and will return to below. In the meantime, critical realists introduce a series of concepts (not all of which are unique to realists) which support and elaborate ontological realism.

According to realists, reality is 'stratified'. This simply means that phenomena in reality have an order of dependency. Things identified in physics (fields, forces, etc.) allow for chemistry, which in turn allow for biology, which in turn allow for society. While there are complexities and nuance to this stratification, it remains the case that without the former in the chain the latter could not be, and it seems plausible to suggest that appropriate explanation allows for different foci based on strata. For example, all relevant aspects of the existence and significance of a factory-farmed chicken cannot be explained merely by biology. At the same time, the chicken does not violate what biology or chemistry allows and it breaks no physical laws. Realists also adopt the concept of 'emergence' and by this they mean that some aspects of reality are produced via the organisation of parts and the organisation leads to new entities and makes possible new powers or capacities not reducible to the parts in isolation. This is closely associated with the idea that reality is a tensed process of change, developing and evolving through time.

With the above as background, critical realists tend to emphasise that states of affairs or events typically arise from a combination of sources termed 'causal mechanisms' (note the terminology does not mean causes are 'mechanistic', causes are sources of outcomes and this can be simply reasons for acting conceived by an agent). Causal mechanism combinations can be decomposed into individual sources of causation, and these typically involve entities that have powers to do things. These powers can be intrinsic to an entity. For example, humans can speak, but do not have sonar, can jump but not fly. They can be acquired from a technology. For example, we have sonar devices and planes. And they can be acquired via a social position which leads to things one must do to fulfil the position and creates both expectations of what to do and new things one can do. For example, a judge has the power to impose a sentence on a person found guilty in a civil or criminal case, a season ticket holder has the right to enter a stadium and attend a football match. It should be obvious that a person can occupy many positions and all seem to involve pre-existing groupings of relationships that define the scope of that position in context and which a person can become part of in given situations. For example, 'student' presupposes a teacher as well as an existing system of education and its infrastructure and purpose within a society.

THE AGENT-STRUCTURE PROBLEM AND THE TMSA

Occupying a position brings us back to the agent-structure problem. The word 'problem' is used because there have been different approaches to the significance of agency and structure. Methodological individualism places the emphasis on the decisive role of agency and treats society as merely an aggregation of individuals (which means society becomes just a convenient word for something which has no substantive existence). Methodological holism places the emphasis on the pervasive influence of structures and treats agents as highly determined by their socialisation. There are also approaches which treat agents and structures as two sides of the same coin.[6] In *The Possibility of Naturalism* Roy Bhaskar provides the original critical realist solution to the problem. 'Society is both the ever-present *condition* (material cause) and continually reproduced *outcome* of human agency' (Bhaskar, 1979, p. 43; for a simple explanation see Buch-Hansen & Nielsen, 2020, p. 54; Collier, 1994, pp. 141–151).

In the 'transformational model of social activity' (TMSA), agents and structures are distinguishable things (not just the same thing from different perspectives). Agents continually interact with structures in society and in so doing typically reproduce those structures. This is usually an unintended consequence of whatever it is they are doing. For example, paying for something reproduces the payments infrastructure and the concept of money. However, many aspects of society involve design, redesign, innovation and invention, which means we are capable of deliberate change, though things may not turn out exactly as intended or only have the effects intended. Despite a focus on 'reproduction', according to critical realists society in its parts and entirety is continually changing in small

---

[6]The main realist making this argument is Margaret Archer. She describes this as a 'central conflation' and argues that if they are simply the same thing from different points of view agents and structures could never interact and thus there could be no theory of interaction in time. She argues that Anthony Giddens's (for whom structure is an 'instantiation' of ideas) work commits this error. See Archer (1995).

and large ways (up to and including transformation in how things are done and how people conceive of themselves). Structures in society are real because they enable and constrain social action. Once they exist they are not, in many cases, easily changed even though they depend on humans for their existence (for their production and reproduction). Society has many different kinds of organisation, which combine systemically; it has laws, rules, many different developed cultures, habits and norms that provide context for agents, but agents are not mere puppets.[7] While we may as agents have multiple social identities and many different roles and contexts within which we are active, we never stop being reflexive beings with a 'first person perspective' able to understand and work on our own conditions of existence—the 'I' who does, related to the 'we' who interact. We have intentions and reasons for acting, long-term goals, plans and desires, the need for belonging, recognition, love and a material body whose emotional states are a continual commentary on our state of mind.[8]

All the above implies society, including its economic aspects, is a tremendously complex and diverse thing. It should also be clear that once one starts to think of any aspect of society along the lines of agent-structure production and reproduction, there can be many different contexts and relevant causal mechanisms in the given case, which combine to produce outcomes or events.[9] It is possible that the same characteristic causes, as a

[7] Note: these are foci for research that may involve possible causal mechanisms. They are not necessarily all 'structures'. Margaret Archer, for example, is critical of the concept of habit and also distinguishes between social structure and culture, which not all realists do. The subject of these debates is not relevant to this chapter. The *Dictionary of Critical Realism* contains short entry essays on all the main concepts and contentions. See Hartwig (2007).

[8] Note: the idea that our bodies have consequences for what we reason about and how we reason is 'embodied reason is a key part of Andrew Sayer's book *Why Things Matter to People*' (Sayer, 2011).

[9] Note, various realists have developed different elaborations of the agent-structure problem after Bhaskar's TMSA. Marger Archer develops her M/M approach, which explicitly introduces interactions in time and explores both 'morphostasis' and 'morphogenesis' (change). See Archer (1995). Bob Jessop argues that Archer's approach is overly sociological and does not include sufficient focus on political economy. His theory is called the 'strategic-relational approach'. See Jessop (2005). Tony Lawson sets out several versions of an evolutionary Population-Variety-Reproduction-Selection (PVRS) model in his book *Reorienting Economics,* but argues that only one of the possible ways of theorising this is compatible with the TMSA and there are definite limits to thinking of a society of agents and structures in terms similar to natural selection (Lawson, 2003). His later work is focused on 'social positioning theory', which, he argues, incorporates the agent structure problem (Lawson, 2019). Dave Elder-Vass introduces the concept of 'norm circles' to explain a key way in which agents act in terms of structure (Elder-Vass, 2012).

combined causal mechanism in an agent-structure situation, produce similar events over time (a simple pattern of outcomes), or that different causes lead to a differently composed combined mechanism that produces a similar set of outcomes or that combinations produce entirely different outcomes. This implies that since reality, unlike a laboratory situation, is not characterised by isolation of single causal sources, it is only ever contingently regular. It may be relatively stable in some ways for some time, but it is never still. Hence, the concept of an open system is in process.[10] This is a convenient point at which to introduce 'epistemological relativism' and then 'judgmental rationality'.

Epistemological Relativism
and Judgemental Rationality

Epistemology refers to 'theory of knowledge', and epistemological relativism just means there can legitimately be several knowledges at the same time. This claim has several components. The world does not reduce to our theories of it, even if some aspects of the world are created from our deliberate activity, beliefs and theories. For example, money and payments systems are core economic aspects of a modern industrial-consumer society, but there are multiple theories of what money is, how it is created, and what its role and significance is. Yet, money is still a functioning component of social reality. A mind-independent reality means that it would be an error to conflate our theories with reality. Realists call this an 'epistemic fallacy'—the reduction of what 'is' to how it is known. Knowledge is a social product and it is always fallible. Moreover, the complexity and diversity of causal mechanisms and the continual scope for change mean two

---

[10] Note: for critical realists the relationship between causal mechanism and events also leads to the concept of 'depth realism'. The standard way to describe depth realism is that there is a difference between the continual existence of mechanisms that produce events, the events produced by combinations of mechanisms and the particular experience of events. Realists refer to these as 'domains' of reality (real, actual and empirical, though there is some debate over the use of this terminology since it seems to invite the inference that the actual and empirical are not real, which is not what is argued—they are all part of reality). See Collier (1994, p. 44). Realists argue that it is usually only in laboratory conditions where a mechanism is isolated that a cause continually produces the same outcome. Event regularity leaves a lot out of the explanation of reality. The test of causality is not regularity in events but powers of things to do things.

things.[11] First, inquiry can be from many different perspectives asking quite different sets of questions and seeking different types of explanation, about reality. I will have more to say about this when we discuss research strategies for sports attendance demand. Second, our knowledge of reality is likely always incomplete. This brings me, finally, to judgemental rationality.

A combination of ontological realism and epistemological relativism might be taken to imply that it is impossible to know anything and that any theory or claim about the world is as good as any other. Critical realists, however, argue that both of these are errors (and familiar ones thanks to some versions of postmodernist theory in the twentieth century and post-truth politics in the twenty-first century). If there is a mind-independent reality then there is something to make truth claims about. Even in social reality, which depends on us as language users, makers and doers for much of its existence, we can refer to how things happen, what has happened and what we intend to happen. It would be an error to dispense with the concept of truth because knowing things has conditions and is difficult.

Critical realists argue that we can have good grounds for taking something to be our best explanation or understanding of how things are (for the moment) based on evidence and reasoned argument. We are capable of considering different arguments and evidence in search of better alternatives and different futures. This does not mean power, mendacity, manipulation and error cease to be concerns, but it would also be an error and actively harmful to dispense with the distinction between knowledge and unfounded belief. For critical realists the absence of absolute truth and certainty does not lead to a world in which nothing is explicable and nothing is justified. This is a false way of posing the problem. Not even the

---

[11] Critical realists also introduce a transitive and intransitive distinction. Knowledge is part of reality, but since knowledge is a social product it is part of a transitive dimension to reality working on intransitive objects (so knowledge is from a point in time working on aspects of reality that do not reduce to the knowledge itself and are more enduring). There is some debate concerning whether this additional terminology is clear or helpful. See Collier (1994, pp. 50–54); Buch-Hansen and Nielsen (2020, pp. 40–41). The best-known discussion of a realist approach to the nature of knowledge is Andrew Sayer's *Method in Social* Science. For a useful bullet point list of issues and insights, see Sayer (1992, pp. 5–6). For Sayer, knowledge is more or less 'adequate'. The realist philosopher Ruth Groff argues that truth is a regulating norm, and we have to make truth claims and seek truth in order for all the other aspects of the knowledge process to have meaning (Groff, 2004).

hardest science makes claims about absolute truth and full certainty, the focus is always on investigation and justification. For critical realists, a further important lesson to be drawn from this is that the methods of inquiry ought to be appropriate to what is under investigation and part of the role of justification is to consider how successful our theories and methods are in multiple ways, including ontology. This is one way in which more adequate theory is developed—seeking ontological consistency.

WHY ALL OF THIS MATTERS FOR SPORTS ECONOMICS AND ATTENDANCE DEMAND

By now you are probably wondering what the point of all of this is. Recall, however, that I began by arguing that for various reasons it is a useful exercise to go back to basics. A lot of those 'basics' have turned out to be, in simplest form and putting aside the new terminology, common sense. I have essentially said the universe predates us as a species; our theory is not the world; social reality is complex, diverse and changing; we have choice but it is constrained and enabled by what already exists and by what is possible, not everything is true and not everything is false and we can work to know the difference. Put this way, the last few pages might seem superfluous or patronising. It is, however, worth going back to basics because it is easy to lose sight of what is assumed in a field of study. In previous chapters I made the point that sports economics as a sub-discipline of economics has adopted much of its theory and methods from the discipline at large (the mainstream). Arguably, this is at odds with some of this 'common sense'.

Attendance demand has adopted and adapted a standard agent. That agent assumes away, at least at first, much of the complex diversity of the agent and their conditions. The main focus of this is to test the strength of separate (isolated) variables of interest on the demand decision, mediated by a calculation and willingness to pay. If we translate this into the concepts developed over the previous subsections, then the focus is on events and on the regular pattern in those events (an event regularity) rather than on the complex, diverse, changing and contingent nature of the mechanisms from which events arise. This presupposes a closed system and takes the focus away from the complexity and diversity of agency *and* structure which underpin events or outcomes (attendance demand leading to attendance itself) in an open system (within a stratified and emergent reality).

To be clear, the claims I am making here are not 'news from nowhere'.[12] Critical realism is not a case of philosophy imposing a point of view. As my previous two chapters should make clear, the starting point is the observed issues and problems of a field of study (in philosophy this is termed an 'immanent critique'). In the case of economics, while few economists today would self-identify as positivists, the focus on event regularity is clearly an enduring positivist legacy. The result is a problem of mismatch in ontology (the 'theory of being' inherent in assumptions, theory, use of methods and aims). The existence of this mismatch is only exposed by going back to basics and it is only by going back to basics that building an alternative can make sense. Moreover, in the case of sports economics the mismatch is not surprising. Sports economics is already on one side of a divide and economists are not encouraged to think about fundamentals. Few are exposed to philosophy and methodology as part of their education and there is a great emphasis on developing a skillset focused on the received toolkit, especially analytical statistics. This leads to a mentality of 'this is what economists do'. Put another way, there has been little pressure to justify theory and methods in ontological terms (what it is to be an economist has been sufficiently settled that judgemental rationality has never been a major *ontological* issue for sports economics and the possibility and need for an alternative—on the other side of a dividing line—has gained little or no attention).

To reiterate, the treatment of the agent does not fit well with ontological realism and a developed approach to the agent-structure problem. I would argue it makes more sense to start from a focus on identifying and exploring mechanisms in an agent-structure framework. Among other things this has the significant attraction that while current theory in sports economics encounters multiple problems if regularities are *not* found, a critical realist approach can accommodate relative stability, but is comfortable with diversity and irregularity in both cause and outcome—it is a non-atomistic open systems perspective. Moreover, given that sports attendance demand is quintessentially social, involving many different considerations that seem very far from those allowed by the standard economic agent, a critical realist informed research strategy seems especially appropriate. Before sketching out a strategy focused on sports attendance

[12] The phrase is taken from Morgan (2016a, 2016b). 'Immanent critique' just means philosophy starts from existing debates and claims and seeks to draw lessons from them and to reconcile issues. The agent-structure problem is a good example.

demand, I first turn to behavioural economics for inspiration regarding the concept of an agent and agency. My main focus is Daniel Kahneman and the reason for this will become clearer later.

BEHAVIOURAL ECONOMICS: STARTING POINTS

Daniel Kahneman was awarded the 'Sveriges Riksbank Prize in Economic Sciences in Memory of Alfred Nobel' in 2002. He shared the prize with Vernon L. Smith, one of the founders of experimental economics. According to the organisation, Kahneman was awarded the prize 'for having integrated insights from psychological research into economic science, especially concerning human judgment and decision-making under uncertainty'.[13] Kahneman's best-known work in economics was undertaken jointly with Amos Tversky. In particular, 'Judgment Under Uncertainty: Heuristics and Biases' (Tversky & Kahneman, 1974) and 'Prospect Theory: An Analysis of Decisions Under Risk' (Kahneman & Tversky, 1979). Together these two works have helped to set the scene for the integration of behavioural economics into the mainstream. For example, as of February 2024 according to Google Scholar, the Prospect Theory article (across its various reprints and inclusion in edited collections) had been cited more than 82,000 times.

In terms of economics, Kahneman and Tversky's main target was expected utility theory (EUT) and the concept of the rational agent (see Karni, 2016). EUT is a main variant of the type of agent I discuss in detail in my previous chapters. According to Kahneman and Tversky, 'modern decision theory (Finetti, 1968; Savage, 1954) regards subjective probability as the quantified opinion of an idealised person' (Tversky & Kahneman, 1974, p. 1130).[14] For Tversky and Kahneman, as the phrase 'idealised'

---

[13] Visit: https://www.nobelprize.org/prizes/economic-sciences/2002/kahneman/biographical/ Note: it is probably worth stating that the term uncertainty has a variety of meanings (see Dow, 2012a). In economics, John Maynard Keynes and Frank Knight distinguish uncertainty from risk. Risk allows for a quantitative measure and probability calculation. Fundamental uncertainty is a situation where one might think things are possible, but there is no possibility of an accurate probability calculation. However, many economists confuse these two terms and it is not always clear that behavioural economists mean uncertainty in Keynes's sense. Expected utility theory tends to conflate risk and uncertainty. See also later footnote mentioning Savage's second postulate in the context of subjective probability.

[14] Essentially expected utility theory assumes that subjective probability determines preferences but preferences converge on optimal outcomes over time—it is possible to maximise utility in the world. Behind this, however, 'there is a similarity in the programs of economics

indicates, there is no such person. They then set out to establish an alternative using experiment rather than assertion and assumption. However, the main focus was to use the standard rational agent as a benchmark and design an experiment to test whether in fact a person conformed to that benchmark under given conditions. This becomes a situation of heuristics with an ever-increasing list of biases. Prospect Theory resituates this by introducing a different approach to cognition. A standard rational economic agent calculates and makes use of available information to optimise.[15] There is a convergence on optimal or maximising outcomes. In Prospect Theory, in contrast, the agent continually frames decisions as 'risky prospects and gambles'—rather than a certainty of outcome or statistically contrived convergence on an optimal outcome (as a prospect). The agent develops different 'cognitively efficient' ways to cope with the absence of certainty and incomplete information. Agents engage in a two-stage process of simplification and evaluation and then develop various ways to come to decisions. Decisions are made with recognition of the limits of cognition.

The use of experiment to identify new biases or to explore the existence of known forms of biases in new contexts, such as sports economics, has become a standard part of mainstream economics. However, there are

and classical stimulus-response behaviourism: both approaches seek to predict behaviour from a specification of its circumstances' (Kahneman et al., 1986, p. 298). While Kahneman acknowledges that the rational-actor model has some relevance in restricted circumstances of individual self-interest he points out, for example, 'The rational agent model has more questionable consequences in the domain of policy because the assumption that individuals are rational in the pursuit of their interests has an ideological colouring and policy implications that many would view as unfortunate. If individuals are rational, there is no need to protect them against their own choices. At the extreme, no need for Social Security or for laws that compel motorcycle riders to wear helmets. It is not an accident that the department of economics at the University of Chicago, one of the most illustrious in the world, is known both for its adherence to a strict version of the rational actor model and for very conservative politics.' Interview with Jesse Singal (2013). See also Machina (2008).

[15] Note: the claim that the agent has complete information is slightly misleading for EUT and there is more to this in terms of statistics. Decisions are made 'under uncertainty' but uncertainty allows for well-defined probability and utility functions. Savage's second postulate (a 'sure thing principle') and various other aspects of the approach allow preference behaviour to reveal probability and the utility function (see Mongin, 1997). There is considerable debate regarding EUT and decision theory. The intricacies of this are not relevant to my argument.

various strands of behavioural economics.[16] In addition to heuristics and biases and Prospect Theory, there is also work on 'bounded rationality'. To be clear, this term has several interpretations, some of which predate Kahneman and Tversky. In the 1950s, Herbert Simon originally defined bounded rationality as 'rational choice that takes into account the cognitive limitations of the decisionmaker – limits of both knowledge and computational capacity' (summarised in Simon, 1987). Simon's work predates modern formalism and more recently economists self-identifying as behavioural economists have sought to develop Simon's work along more mathematical and modelling lines. It is arguable how far this is consistent with Simon's intent, but what is important is that it differs from Kahneman and Tversky's approach.[17] While Kahneman and Tversky recognise cognitive limitation, they do not restrict their concept to limited computational capacity; instead, they suggest agents develop systemised ways of coping with this limitation (heuristics and biases, etc.).

However, while Kahneman and Tversky did not use the phrase 'bounded rationality' in their early work, they did start to make reference to it later in order to accommodate the growing use of the term. In any case, it is important to note that behavioural economics has developed and diversified over the years. Today there are numerous debates regarding what its status is in the field and the degree of progress it represents. This is worth briefly illustrating since it provides scope to look again at behavioural economics in the context of sports economics.

A Step in the Direction of the Path Not Taken by Behavioural Economics

There is considerable debate regarding the scope and adequacy of behavioural economics, much of which tends to be forgotten when its most popular format is appropriated and applied. Erik Angner, for example, well-known author of the bestselling textbook *A Course in Behavioural Economics* (Angner, 2012), recently argued, in a special issue of *Journal of Economic Methodology* devoted to debates in behavioural economics, that

---

[16] Note: while I have focused on Kahneman and Tversky, there is a great deal of work developed from Richard Thaler and Cass Sunstein and I by no means wish to suggest this is irrelevant. See, for example Earl (2018); Heukelom (2014a, 2014b); Altman (2004).

[17] Note: Geoff Hodgson, for example, briefly argues that Heberrt Simon is misunderstood by the mainstream and neglected by heterodox economists (Hodgson, 2019).

we are 'all behavioural economists now' (Angner, 2019). According to Angner, there has been a tacit synthesis between neoclassical economics and behavioural economics and this leans more towards behavioural economics. Despite Angner's interest in 'ontology' (see Angner, 2015), however, this implicitly takes as its premise an argument associated with the 'empirical turn' in economics and that is the idea that economics now has numerous models all of which are appropriate in some circumstance. This is highly debatable.

In any case, as Vladimir Avtonomov and Yuri Avtonomov argue in the same special issue of *Journal of Economic Methodology*, there have been and remain multiple debates regarding the compatibility of psychology and neoclassical economics and its legacy—which they refer to, using a term with a long history in economics, as '*Methodenstreits*' (Avtonomov & Avtonomov, 2019). Fabian Braesemann takes a slightly different approach to make some of the same argument regarding the true impact of behavioural economics. He uses bibliographic data to establish that there has in fact been less importation from psychology via behavioural economics into 'mainstream' economics than is commonly supposed (Braesemann, 2019).

It is probably also worth noting that there are very different points of view on what behavioural economics biggest impacts have been. For example, Sabine Frerichs argues that the accommodation of cognitive behavioural insights into economics has focused mainly on the individual and thus has relatively little to say about sociality (Frerichs, 2019). In contrast, Don Ross argues that economics is converging with sociology but *not* psychology (Ross, 2023). Overall, however, there is general consensus that behavioural economics main impact on economics has remained applications of heuristics and biases to new datasets and situations.[18]

As a last example, Guilhelm Lecouteux provides a humorous take on the dominant approach to behavioural economics and argues that the main approach treats the agent as a malfunctioning individual whom public policy 'fixes' via nudge strategies—a *Homer Economicus* to contrast with traditional *Homo Economicus* (Lecouteux, 2023). Clearly, however,

---

[18] This has been the case for a long time. For example, 'It is important to emphasise that the behavioural economics approach extends rational choice and equilibrium models; it does not advocate abandoning these models entirely' (Holim & Camerer, 2006, p. 308).

diversity and continued debate implies there is scope for different ways of drawing on and developing behavioural economics.[19]

A Quick Reminder of the Relevance of the Argument to Sports Economics

I have previously argued that sports economics has tended to use the most restricted version of behavioural economics focused on simple adoption of tests of well-known biases and application of heuristics (especially loss aversion).[20] If we refer to the terminology we introduced in the sections on critical realism and in my previous chapters on the subject, this suffers from several problems. First, the continual use of the standard agent as a benchmark means that there is little pressure to develop the alternative, and there is instead merely a growing list of heuristics and biases. Second, as anyone familiar with the method of experimentation used to identify heuristic and biases will be aware, the focus is typically on an isolated deviation from the benchmark agent in a controlled environment. Arguably, this is a closure that does not develop the further context of behaviour in an open system. Instead, it presupposes a closed system event regularity situation. This leaves a great deal to say concerning what would happen in an open system situation. Third, there seems to be some confusion over the concept of uncertainty. Controlled experiment focuses on statistical tests and quantifies outcomes. The insight of this is questionable for an open system with multiple causal mechanisms in an agent-structure situation. The focus is again on the regularity of outcome rather than on the contingent sources of action—the mechanisms in an open system where agents are located in terms of structures.

---

[19] As Kahneman notes in his Nobel biographical essay: 'The conclusions that readers drew were often too strong, mostly because existential quantifiers, as they are prone to do, disappeared in the transmission. Whereas we had shown that (some, not all) judgments about uncertain events are mediated by heuristics, which (sometimes, not always) produce predictable biases, we were often read as having claimed that people cannot think straight. The fact that men had walked on the moon was used more than once as an argument against our position. Because our treatment was mistakenly taken to be inclusive, our silences became significant.'

[20] See my first chapter and the survey of *Journal of Sports Economics* and my second chapter and the discussion of the strategies sports economists have used to develop and modify the standard economic agent.

To reiterate, there is scope to look again at behavioural economics and it should be increasingly clear, drawing on my two previous chapters, that this is highly relevant to sports economics. I would argue that there is a less conservative version of Kahneman's work to draw on and which can be placed in an agent-structure and non-atomistic open systems context.[21]

The Path Not Taken in Behavioural Economics and Sports Attendance Demand

Anyone familiar with Kahneman's work and especially with the many essays he has written and interviews he has undertaken since achieving prominence in the social sciences and especially in economics, will know that he is very aware of the limits of his work undertaken with Tversky on heuristics and biases and of the use made of it by others. Kahneman is, in fact, quite candid that although the original intention in the 1974 paper was not directed towards economics, once the decision was made to address economists, much of the focus was a pragmatic choice to achieve publication in economics journals in which it was difficult to get acceptance for work that was outside the existing framework (a point I also made in a previous essay using the example of the problems George Akerlof had with his 'The Market for Lemons').[22] For example, Kahneman states in a sole-authored preface to a joint work with Tversky, 'the theory we constructed was as conservative as possible ... we did not challenge the philosophical analysis of choices' (Kahneman & Tversky, 2000, p. x). According to Kahneman, behavioural economics had to be translated into

---

[21] Note: this could also draw on others such as Veblen, see, for example Stanfield (2023); Dick (2005).

[22] Note: it is important not to traduce Kahneman on his own work and on Tversky. As Kahneman makes clear in his Nobel biographical essay, the 1974 paper was originally conceived as more of a challenge in psychology that was picked up by economists: 'The article soon became a standard reference as an attack on the rational-agent model, and it spawned a large literature in cognitive science, philosophy, and psychology. We had not anticipated that outcome. If we had intended the article as a challenge to the rational model, we would have written it differently, and the challenge would have been less effective. An essay on rationality would have required a definition of that concept, a treatment of boundary conditions for the occurrence of biases, and a discussion of many other topics about which we had nothing of interest to say. The result would have been less crisp, less provocative, and ultimately less defensible. As it was, we offered a progress report on our study of judgment under uncertainty, which included much solid evidence.' The significance of the work developed later (Kahneman, 2002).

a language of concepts economists could understand and methods they were prepared to work with. This, ironically, has biased its development ever since (though Kahneman probably wouldn't put it quite like this and continues to be positive—with some reservations—about what economists have achieved).

It is important to note, moreover, that while Kahneman and Tversky came from broadly similar disciplinary backgrounds, and Kahneman is effusive in his praise for Tversky and their working relationship in his Nobel biographical essay, it is widely acknowledged the two constituted an 'odd couple'. Furthermore, Tversky was mainly interested in a standard analytical statistical tests approach to models of psychology and Kahneman was not.[23] Tversky's methods seem to have dominated what economists have made of their joint work. Floris Heukelom provides some useful background on this in *Behavioural Economics: A History* (Heukelom, 2014a).

In their previous separate work, Tversky worked with the normative-descriptive method of Ward Edwards and Kahneman focused on the psychology of mistakes—getting it wrong and not even realising it (Heukelom, 2014a). For Edwards, a normative method starts from how a person should behave (a set of assumptions that may or may not be well-founded), while a descriptive approach seeks to find out how they really behave. Tversky, following Edwards, uses the normative standard as a benchmark to test in experiment what agents actually do.[24] The emphasis is on beginning from the benchmark and on models and quantified tests. In contrast, Kahneman was more interested in why the agent can't behave that way. Kahneman was most interested in the 'how, when and why the cognitive machinery fails to act' when compared to the benchmark (Heukelom, 2014a, p. 110).[25] Kahneman's concerns extended to a variety of related issues that provide reasons and context for the nature of action such as

---

[23] See the Nobel biographical essay for Kahneman's praise for Tversky (Kahneman, 2002).

[24] Tversky typifies what behavioural psychologists have made of Edwards's work. The method starts from what axioms of behaviour would be necessary for a rational outcome and this becomes the standard by which the deviation from them is measured. This is an odd method if one thinks about what it is achieving—it questions notional axioms empirically while retaining them despite this. See Heukelom (2014a, p. 97). This is simply a different way of stating there is a null hypothesis to reject and the null hypothesis has a very standardised form.

[25] According to Heukelom (2014a, p. 110), 'the key to understanding Kahneman's psychology lies in his conviction that human beings often make cognitive errors.' It is the frequency that is significant here, that is it is a *normal* state not aberration.

intuition, while Tversky's strength was experimental design and extraction of a finding (which we might describe as an isolated regularity). Overall, Kahneman's perspective seems far more conducive to placing the agent outside of controlled situations to consider broader issues in more complex uncontrolled settings.[26] This I would suggest helps to place his work and then sports attendance demand on the other side of the divide in economics.

Perhaps the best place to start in making the case is with Kahneman's popular bestseller *Thinking Fast and Slow* (Kahneman, 2011). This book cemented Kahneman's reputation as more than simply Tversky's lesser partner (Tversky and Kahneman did not work together for some time after 1983, Tversky went to Stanford and was for some period until his death in 1996 recipient of the greater acclaim).[27] In *Thinking Fast and Slow* it is very clear that Kahneman's contribution was not simply reducible to Tversky's. In the book Kahneman is less constrained by models and tests and free to focus on underlying explanations and issues of context as well as caveats regarding limits of the main focus of his joint work with Tversky.

For our purpose the key point to make is that Kahneman introduces a set of concepts and insights which add detail and nuance to the psyche of the agent in terms of how decisions are made.[28] However, he is also quite clear that this is insufficient to explain what occurs in real situations beyond the laboratory. I would argue that this implies the need to place his experimentally observed agent within an agent-structure framework (which in

[26] According to Heukelom (2014a), Kahneman and Tversky worked with the problem of Bayesian updating which is central to the process inherent to rational maximisation by an agent in expected utility theory, but Kahneman was less convinced than Tversky that deviations were systematic and predictable. This implies that Kahneman and Tversky, despite their collaboration, had different concepts of the role of probability and uncertainty. For Kahneman intuition, etc., places a question mark over the quantification and regularity found in standard model approaches to behavioural economics. He perhaps had a more Keynesian or Knightian concept of uncertainty.

[27] Note: I am not claiming that Kahneman repudiated his earlier work or moved away from experimentation. Rather, he thought differently over his career about what it achieved. In his later work he also went on to explore decision-making and belief in religion, politics and finance.

[28] For further examples, see *New Challenges to the Rationality Assumption* (Kahneman, 1991). Kahneman recognises that there are many dimensions to utility (both formal decision utility and multiple forms of experienced hedonistic utility). He sets aside behaviourism (the philosophy of science) and argues that the complexity of real experiences involves combinations not represented by formal decision theory.

turn is within an open system non-atomistic perspective focused on causal mechanisms), rather than simply refer to isolated findings in laboratory situations which result in determination of generic bias (e.g. while a situation may be describable as yet another case of loss aversion, this tells one little about the fuller reality of choices and situations).

Thinking Fast and Slow divides into five parts, but its most important contribution is the distinction between System 1 and System 2 thinking (see Kahneman, 2011, pp. 19–105). Each involves 'traits and dispositions'. System 1 covers decisions in situations where the agent responds on the basis of recursive behaviour, habit or routine and does so more or less immediately and without further conscious thought (for summation see Kahneman, 2011, p. 105). It is important to note that while System 1 decision-making is typically effortless and characterised by a lack of sense of voluntarily control, it is still *learned* behaviour. There is a wide range of standard examples in different circumstances. A person with significant schooling does not think before responding to 2+2 with the answer 4. A driver travelling by car to a familiar and frequent destination (home) will not be able to recall exactly what they did to get there. In other instances an agent learns to use their emotions (their feelings) as sources of response or draws on deep background learned response and thinks of this later as 'intuition'. Clearly, all these would be different based on what one learned and thus would vary historically, by place and circumstance and culturally. This implies a role for *socialisation* and for enculturation which reduction to identification of a generic bias or similar approach simply misses.

System 2 thinking involves situations where deliberation is required. These situations are encountered less frequently or are of greater complexity or consequence. This means decisions are reached more slowly and require conscious effort—attention is required. As with System 1, System 2 covers a wide range of possible circumstances. For example, Kahneman discusses 'check the validity of a complex logical argument', but most importantly for our purpose 'monitor the appropriateness of your behaviour in a social situation' (Kahneman, 2011, p. 22).[29] This leads to the same conclusion as the one I drew for System 1, an adequate understanding of how an agent has acted requires fuller understanding of socialisation and enculturation. Put another way, it requires specification of the circumstances in which a decision was made and this essentially is an agent-

---

[29] For the complete list see Kahneman (2011, p. 22), but for full discussion see again Kahneman (2011, pp. 19–105).

structure framework (again within an open system non-atomistic perspective focused on causal mechanisms).[30]

It should also be kept in mind that Kahneman is clear that his distinction between System 1 and System 2 is based on metaphor (Kahneman, 2011, p. 13). The distinction is not intended to imply thinking has hard and fast divisions regarding 'mental life'. For Kahneman, while System 1 has greater influence over everyday conduct than we like to think (since we like to think of ourselves as creatures of careful reflexive reason), 'System 2 has some ability to change the way System 1 works, by programming the normally automatic functions of attention and memory' (Kahneman, 2011, p. 23).[31] In any case, agents are *not* segmented or fixed (reified) repositories of separated functions but rather a multiplicity of facets that evolve through learning and respond to context. The mental life of the agent presents as a coherent singular entity active in different contexts and developing through time. This has important implications. On the one hand, society is not just a background of situations that an agent finds themselves acting in. Enculturation and socialisation by context, time and place must surely change who a person is and how they are in terms of how they act—an agent has what philosophers call a 'phenomenology'. This is a point I drew attention to without using this phrase in a previous chapter with reference to John Davis on social identity and personal identity. On the other hand, the significance of decision-making is not just internal to the encultured and socialised psyche of the agent. What an agent can choose to do has definite enablement and constraint depending on the structured situations they find themselves active within in contexts, time and place. As Kahneman states in his Nobel biographical essay:

---

[30] Note: there are many other aspects to Kahneman's argument over the five parts in the book which could also be of interest. For example, his concept of 'two selves'. He identifies an 'experiencing self' and a 'remembering self'. The former is moment to moment and the latter is reflective. However, in recollection the past is subject to new narratives and overlays which create an evolving meaning out of one's memory. It is not a simple absolute recall of what has happened or a set of fragments. This also leads to the idea of 'focusing illusion', events or aspects of life can take on disproportionate focus and significance.

[31] 'In the picture that emerges from recent research, the intuitive System 1 is more influential than your experience tells you, and it is the secret author of many of the choices and judgments you make' (Kahneman, 2011, p. 13).

The fact that we had written nothing about the role of social factors in judgment was taken as an indication that we thought these factors were unimportant. I suppose that we could have prevented at least some of *these misunderstandings*, but the cost of doing so would have been too high. (Kahneman, 2002, emphasis added)

And as he put it earlier even than that:

Significant decisions are made in a social and emotional context, rather than in experimental anonymity ... The segregation of cognitive and psychophysical from emotional and social factors in the study of choice is in a large part an accident of research traditions. (Kahneman, 1991, p. 145, emphasis added)

To reiterate, that accident seems to have become the basis of behavioural economics assimilation into the mainstream. I would argue that Kahneman's agent is more appropriately placed on the other side of the divide in economics. This opens up the possibility of a more expansive research strategy for sports attendance demand which both moves beyond the standard economic agent modified from neoclassical economics and takes the agent 'of decision' (as the phrase is used in behavioural economics) beyond experimental situations and isolations.

A CRITICAL REALIST BEHAVIOURAL ECONOMICS HYBRID FOR RESEARCH ON SPORTS ATTENDANCE DEMAND

In the introduction to this chapter I drew attention to a divide in economics and suggested that one side (the dominant side) prefers a precise specification of an agent's actions and decision-making scope (tests of the strength of isolated variables of interest, etc.) and the other side works with the diverse contexts, motivations, practices and reasoning of agents— the sociality of the experience and its consequences. I set out the initial question, 'if we *don't* start from the standard economic agent, what does a theory of and research strategy for sports attendance demand look like?' So far I have 'gone back to basics' to provide a background theory, drawing on critical realism, whose focus is the identification of combinations of causal mechanisms in an agent-structure, non-atomistic, open systems framework and I have suggested that Kahneman's work on the agent can be resituated within this framework. While there is obviously a great deal more that could be done to develop and defend what I have written, I do not have the space to do so in this chapter. However, I would suggest that I have said sufficient to at least make the case plausible and I would add that the strongest point in favour of what I have written so far is that the concepts and arguments I have provided constitute an explicit justification of theory and method. Not only is this something that sports economics typically lacks, but also the ontological case I have made (for the other side of a divide) has the significant attraction, as noted in the introduction, that its theory and methods are *not at odds* with what we observe regarding the phenomena under investigation (it works equally well with relative stability and with the contingency, variability and irregularity of the social world of which sports attendance is a small part). I take this as sufficient for me to move on and discuss a research strategy consistent with my argument so far.

For critical realists the appropriate overall approach to investigation and methods, which works with multiple causal mechanisms in open systems, is referred to as 'retroduction'. According to Lawson:

> The essential mode of inference drawn upon in sciences is neither induction nor deduction. Rather it is one that can be styled *retroduction* or *abduction* or 'as if' reasoning. This consists in the movement, on the basis of analogy and metaphor amongst other things, from a conception of some phenomenon of interest to a conception of some totally different type of thing, mechanism, structure or condition that is responsible for the given phenomenon. If deduction is illustrated by the move from the *general* claim that 'all ravens are black' to the *particular* inference that the next one seen will be black, and induction by the move from the *particular* observation of numerous black ravens to the *general* claim that 'all ravens are black', retroductive or abductive reasoning is indicated by a move from the observation of numerous black ravens to a theory of a mechanism intrinsic (and perhaps also extrinsic) to ravens which disposes them to being black. It is a movement, paradigmatically, from a surface phenomenon to some 'deeper' causal thing ... [and this includes] statements elucidating structures and their characteristic modes of activity. (Lawson, 2003, p. 145)[32]

[32] Note: the broader context of the quote from Lawson is a discussion of why method needs to come to terms with the complexity and contingency of social reality (an economy). Events have causes and causes are not necessarily observable (the socialisation and enculturation which help explain why an agent will pay to attend a sports event are not observed). Hence, the need for inference and creative approach to evidence. See also later comment on 'demi-regularity'.

With this in mind the obvious question to ask is what are the relevant aspects of sports attendance demand which might help us understand and explain it—drawing inferences about combinations of causal mechanisms based on the characteristics of agency and the structures in terms of which agents make decisions. This is quite different than presupposing the standard agent, assuming preferences are given, and then trying to fit the reality of sports attendance demand to that agent. In my second chapter I set out in detail a participant observation ethnographic 'day at the football', posed the question, 'is it reasonable to think that the person who attended a sports event of the kind described [in that ethnography] becomes some version of the standard economic agent at the point of purchase of the ticket that secures attendance?' and then discussed many of the things which might influence attendance demand in a section titled 'what does it mean or what is it worth?'. We can draw on this material as a starting point to outline various lines of research (though I am going to turn from Preston North End to Manchester United below for reasons that will become obvious—apologies to fellow North End fans).[33]

---

[33] As a brief reminder: my identification with Preston North End formed (forms) an important part of my self-image. Identifying with a team is an integral part of my psychological health (and angst, since I suffer with the community of fans and this is part of the sense of belonging that keeps one attending) and part of my social identity. However, such mechanisms work alongside others such as social connectedness. Attendance at matches was a key part of maintaining relationships with friends and family. For me, spending time amongst close friends was a key driver in the choice to attend. Furthermore, the sharing of such experiences reenforced bonds through the sharing of emotional highs and lows connected to the matches themselves. The bonds developed over time, their importance grew as friendships evolved and deepened. As such, the mechanisms evolved—hence, in my case contingency, diversity and multiplicity of attachments driving attendance, and I might add here, since I did not mention it in the previous chapter, these demonstrated stronger and weaker significance at different times of the season. For example, since my friendship with Paul and Chris did not really extend beyond football, mechanisms of attachment were weaker at the start of the season and strengthened as the season progressed. When the season ended, these bonds weakened as I spent no further time with them. This contrasted with my relationship with my brother who I spend considerable time with as a friend, including social events outside of the match-day environment and frequent excursions outside of the season. In any case, my main point is that these types of considerations help to explain the person in a position (who becomes an agent) who makes the decision to attend. See later discussions. Note: I am not suggesting any of this material will come as much of a surprise to sociologists of sport; my point is that they sit awkwardly with sports economics. For background on ethnographic research, see Atkinson (2016).

The first thing to highlight is that the discussion in the previous chapter and in this one makes it clear that research must be sensitive to contingency and heterogeneity. Put another way, it ought to start from what makes sports attendance 'what it observably is'. As should be clear from the ethnography, this implies starting from what makes the agent who they are that then makes the decisions that the agent makes. This is a step back from the typical focus in sports economics. In typical attendance demand research, pricing is the focal point for the decision and the framework assumes optimising utility or meeting preferences of the individual are associated with what an agent is 'willing to pay' to attend. In the previous chapter, however, I made the point that for a fan the presumption is to attend and one needs reasons *not* to do so.[34] 'What do I need to do in order to be able to afford to attend?' is a quite different logic than the standard agent works with. For research purposes it raises the question 'why does a fan think that way?' and this is a version of '*why* is the agent willing to pay?' (and why will they *continue* to pay rather than merely what are they willing to pay). This leads to several different lines of inquiry. It leads to an interest in what influences the way an agent thinks and it leads to an interest in the difference between types of agent, since not all will be fans (and not all fans are equally committed). Moreover, it leads to an interest in some of the ongoing tensions that influence not just identity as a particular kind of agent but identification with the significant other—the sports team (the 'club' etc.) which is the object of identification, as well as the relevant 'we' who become important relational groupings for the purposes of attendance (kinship, friendship, familiarity groupings and the roles undertaken, obligations accepted and so on). This in turn leads to an interest in the ongoing dynamics of reproduction and change constituting agency and structure.

Consider Manchester United football club for a moment. United were bought by the Glazer family in a controversial debt-leveraged buyout in 2005. The club have a large number of season ticket holders and a global

---

[34] Note: affordability is a well-documented issue in sports research. For example, see Fink et al. (2002); Lee (2009); Hong (2008). If we return to the ethnography, we all had quite different employment, income and household situations which constituted different financial constraints. However, we all approached those constraints in the same way insofar as paying to attend took precedence over some other things (not everything) and little of this had anything to do with a conscious sense of measurable preferences or optimisation. There was, however, a difference between holding a season ticket and paying the extra for cup and away games.

fanbase, a stadium (Old Trafford) with a capacity of **74,000**, an active corporate spectator hosting business, a retail outlet at the stadium and other outlets in cities around the world, an online merchandising operation, their own TV channel, a heavy social media presence and a carefully curated history focused on a tradition stemming from the 'Busby Babes' era and the Munich air disaster, as well as a recent track record (until about a decade ago) of dominance in the Premier League. United very obviously attract a wide variety of attendees and spectators (in-person and via TV, etc.): the season ticket holder (in the main stands or the family stand), the on-the-day attendee (which disguises a whole host of hoops one might have to jump through to be eligible for a ticket—membership, accrued points or credits, etc.), the corporate dinner-hosted spectator (who may have no personal relation to the club), the fanatical overseas supporter who has bought a holiday package that includes a ticket to see United.[35]

Attending a match at United is a very different agent-structure interaction than it would have been 40 years ago.[36] Moreover, it is a very different

[35] Note: ticketing policy is a fascinating area of interest. See, for example Yilmaz et al. (2023) who discuss in detail, in an American context, technology, data and markets. More generally, ticketing policy has tended to change as club ownership and governance have changed. In many top-tier professional sports, many clubs have demand for tickets far in excess of available supply. Liverpool FC, for example, have a waiting list of over 70,000 fans for season tickets and this has been closed since 2011, meaning no new additions can be made to the waiting list (liverpoolfc.com). In order to manage demand, it has become common or fans to be required to acquire 'credits' or 'points' for attendance. In lower-tier clubs, although demand is generally less than full capacity, there have still been changes in eligibility for tickets, often related to security issues. It is also notable that as clubs move closer to elite status and as capacity issues arise, clubs create rules that bind the fan to them using ever more stringent eligibility requirements. For example, attendance at UEFA Champions League games might require evidence of attendance at (otherwise poorly attended) League Cup games. Clubs are manifestly exploiting fans to maximise revenues and smooth demand. Clubs are not monopolies in the traditional sense, but they have considerable affinity power if not market power over their 'consumers'. This has elements of ritual servitude—labour (attendance) one must endure (a rainy Wednesday night watching youth team players struggle against some 'lesser club' in an early round of a cup …).

[36] And very different than it was at the time Arthur Hopcraft wrote *The Football Man: People and Passions in Soccer* in the late 1960s. The book is set out in sections dealing among others with players, managers, referees, directors, fans and the future (Hopcraft, 2013/1968). But while much has changed Hopcraft's introduction still resonates: 'The point about football in Britain is that it is not just a sport that people take to like cricket or tennis or running long distances. It is inherent in the people. It is built into the urban psyche … It is not a phenomenon it is an everyday matter … The way we play the game, organize it and reward it reflects the kind of community we are.'

kind of experience in some ways than the ethnographic 'day at the foot-ball' I set out for Preston North End in my previous chapter, since the latter does not fall into the elite sport category. This illustrates that questions such as 'why does a fan think that way?' and '*why* is the agent willing to pay?' will involve some significant variation. In the case of United this is likely entangled in a more overt tension between the commodification of a football club as a corporate-driven profitmaking entity and a well-documented resentment regarding the role of the Glazers as owners (and a separation between supporting the Team and Club and supporting its corporate structure), all of which makes it more difficult to maintain the necessary fiction that seems essential to competitive team sports that are also businesses but depend on supporters (and that is that the business is 'beside the point'—despite that fans may also place heavy economic and commercial demands on their club and criticise a lack of 'investment').

Following on from the United example and with the arguments I have been making in mind, it should be clear that it is an open question how different attendance is (as a precursor to *why* pay or why *continue* to pay) in different contexts. Is Manchester City significantly different than United or are, given the very different league and ownership structures, Bayern Munich or Barcelona?[37] No doubt you can think of others based on any sport you care to name or are familiar with. What I would say, however, is that sticking with a standard economic agent won't help answer such questions. It is, to reiterate, via inference to causal mechanisms that they are addressed. I would also emphasise that heterogeneity is not anarchy. Arguably, the core of the experience is similar. In the case of sports attendance demand, there is socialisation, enculturation, identification and affinity, all focused on an uncertain experience that is both a form of entertainment and involves the reproduction of belonging. If we think about what this implies then several questions seem central as ways to situate research and I summarise them below:

1. What is the nature of agency? What categories or types of agent might agency decompose into, what matters to the agent and helps to *make them* the kind of agent who does what that agent does and thinks as that agent thinks, since this prefigures any given act of agency, including the decision to attend?

[37] Ownership is another fascinating area—investment funds buying sports clubs as financial instruments, 'sportswashing', etc.

2. What is the degree of agency in any given structured situation and how do agents change in relation to their changing environment, while in turn, helping to shape that environment?

It should be clear that this is a focus on how decisions are made rather than merely what decision is made, and this is more than simply 'cognitively efficient' heuristics to cope with information shortcomings and which lead to biases. What we 'do' is not a bias, it is part of who we are.[38] To return to a point I made earlier, this kind of approach has explanatory purchase irrespective of whether events are regular and irrespective of the existence of diversity and change in agents and the structures that they are engaged in. Questions 1 and 2 return us to:

3. What are the causal mechanisms that might account for events as they are? What accounts for the willingness to pay, relationships to affordability and so on? This, again, focuses attention on the characteristic socialisation and enculturation that occurs; the specific institutions, and the social identities one might adopt and cultural practices that tie agents into sports attendance.

As a final point I might also add that both System 1 and System 2 thinking fit readily into this kind of approach.[39] The same might be said of the various other possible resources I have mentioned in my previous work.[40]

[38] Note: it is perhaps also worth noting that socialisation can have many complexities. If a parent supports a non-elite team, it is not uncommon for their children to resist wholehearted adoption of that team and combine it with an elite one.

[39] For example, the well-known critical realist Andrew Sayer uses *Thinking Fast and Slow* as an example of how agents combine habit and reflexive deliberative thinking. See the interview Sayer and Morgan (2022). I might also add, given that Kahneman recognises that people apply a range of decision-making strategies, we can adapt Kahneman's concepts of the remembering and experiencing self (e.g. from his focus on well-being): (1) 'Remembered utility' drawing on grudges, local rivalries, media build-ups and many other forms of discussion that inflate expectations of a sports event. (2) 'Experienced utility' in the form of moment-to-moment fan participation whose cumulative sense tends to diverge from (1). One can also distinguish between real-time utility of the event and residual utility from the event, augmented by subsequent related activity TV debates, interviews, newspaper reports, poring over league position, leading into anticipation of the next event (as well as associated interests such as Fantasy League participation). This, of course, diverges from standard expected utility work.

[40] Edward Fullbrook on inter-subjectivity and intra-subjectivity, Mary Wrenn on 'mental models', John Davis on social identity, and Michael Bratman on shared and collective intentionality.

In any case, there will always be some 'rationale' or reasoning process and it is from this that one might 'retroduce' causal mechanisms. The point I would highlight, however, is that no single cause is likely to be significant or decisive, either for any given agent or decision or for all agents all of the time. I now turn finally to the question of methods we might adopt to pursue this kind of research strategy.

MULTI AND MIXED METHODS, TRIANGULATION AND INTERDISCIPLINARITY

The first point to make is that there are no 'realist methods' (just methods anyone can adopt and realists use), but there are well-established arguments from realists regarding use of methods (which inform a 'methodology') and there is no need for us to start from scratch. Andrew Sayer's *Method in Social Science: A Realist Approach*, Bob Carter and Caroline New's edited text *Making Realism Work,* and the collection *Applied Economics and the Critical Realist Critique,* edited by Paul Downward, provide useful material.[41] As I mentioned in my first chapter, Downward's name appears in the original editorial launching the *Journal of Sports Economics* and over the years he has gone on to be a prominent figure in the field (notably as co-author of *Sports Economics*), an accomplished econometrician, but also an advocate of heterodox economics.[42] Drawing on these works, especially the last, realists take as their starting point that there is a need to respect ontological realism and epistemological relativism while striving for judgemental rationality and that methods ought to be appropriate to the object of investigation.

The last of these commitments raises an obvious flag for many economists. The tendency to start from a core of universally applied concepts, modified in the light of a sub-discipline, and to focus heavily on datasets and econometric models and tests means that economists are often constrained by what they can do before focusing on what the phenomena suggest. This is another way of drawing attention to a point I have made several times before about the problems sports economics and research on

---

[41] See Sayer (1992); Carter and New (2004); Downward and Mearman (2003). Paul Edwards, Joe O'Mahoney and Steve Vincent's edited text *Studying Organizations Using Critical Realism: A Practical Guide* also contains some useful essays (Edwards et al., 2014).

[42] See Downward et al. (2009) and more recently the edited text *The Sage Handbook of Sports Economics* (Downward et al., 2019).

attendance demand have encountered (since many may have felt there was no option but to meet expectations and others may not have been aware of the problems and alternatives). It is also a reminder that a different methodology places study of sports economics attendance demand on the other side of a divide. This is by no means to suggest that sports economics lacks a focus on developing methods. For example, *The Handbook of Sports Economics Research* illustrates the state of the art (see Fizel, 2017/2006), while *Behavioural Sports Economics: A Research Companion* does something similar for the range of possible applications of experiment (Altman et al., 2022).[43]

Moving on, realists tend to advocate multi and mixed methods, since this is consistent with both working from what seems appropriate to the object of study and with epistemological relativism.[44] As the term implies, multi-method research draws on several methods. These, however, could all be of similar type. A researcher, for example, might use structured and semi-structured interviews, recordings of deliberative public forums or guided discussion groups, and participant observation, as well as surveys and questionnaires. These might be focused as case studies or more generalised to a phenomena, but all of them would be categorised as 'qualitative methods'. The typical intent of qualitative methods is to gain insight into meaningful activity—thoughts and feelings which form attitudes, beliefs, expectations, intentions and so on, and which invite reflection on practices, habits or routines that may exist and invite opinion on the context of activity. It seems clear, based on everything I have argued in this and previous chapters, that if you want to understand and explain sports attendance demand, and especially socialisation and enculturation,

---

[43] The Fizel (2017/2006) handbook first divides its subject matter by different team sports and then provides chapters on standard issues: demand, competitive balance, theory of contests, etc. In contrast, Altman et al. (2022) focus on well-known issues researched in behavioural economics in a sports context (heuristics, reference points, incentives, etc.). For work on attendance demand from the latter, see Schreyer (2022).

[44] Note: to avoid confusion 'what is appropriate to the object of study' is not an 'empiricist' claim that we have unmediated access to the world and the world just 'tells us how it is'. It is the reasonable insight that experience of research tends to throw up problems which make it clear as time passes which methods are more or less appropriate to a situation. Many realists use metaphor to explain this (Lawson likes to talk about not using hammers to cut grass or hair). For this to happen though, there needs to be lively critique of methods and an interest in establishing explanatory success (some might call this replication and confirmation, though this language has its own history and problems—the emphasis it places on event regularity, etc.) and ontological coherence. See Danermark comments later.

qualitative methods are indispensable, and use of diverse qualitative methods advisable.

A strategy using qualitative methods is, of course, more complex than just 'ask supporters, watch supporters, try being a supporter'. Attendance demand has many possible sources of influence based on context. There are issues that some but not others will have greater insight into and whose knowledge or expertise warrants particular focus:[45]

- Experts in the economy of football (its metrics and trends).
- Experts in how sports clubs market to supporters.
- Those who engage in community outreach and community building.
- Those responsible for the strategies clubs use to curate tradition and manage the difficult balancing act between a commodified entertainment and framing an ongoing relation in terms of some version of 'experiencing partisan sporting spirit' that might feed into fandom (and for which the term public relations seems insufficient—I am by no means suggesting clubs tend to get this right—ineffectiveness is, of course, a legitimate focus of research).
- The sports-legal experts who provide advice and who develop ties to government, governance and sports administration (which itself demands an expertise in organisation, institutions, law and evolving rules—it would be naïve to assume sports clubs are passive components of markets, and it seems more reasonable to investigate whether and how they seek to shape the landscape they are active in).

No doubt there are others, but this list is sufficient to make the point—much of this is discussed (and with greater range and detail) in *Routledge Handbook of Qualitative Research in Sport and Exercise*, albeit the main focus is participation (Smith & Sparkes, 2019).

Moving on, not all qualitative methods lead only to qualitative techniques of evidence formation. Surveys and questionnaires, for example, allow patterns to be identified and provide an opportunity for statistics to be produced. NVivo and other packages also allow patterns to be identified from interview material. (Economists also often forget that many of the datasets they work with derive originally from someone somewhere answering questions and filling in surveys from which counts can be

---

[45] See, for example, Parnell et al. (2022); Bond et al. (2022); Power et al. (2020).

derived). This brings me to mixed methods via quantitative methods.[46] Mixed methods research combines different types of method—quantitative and qualitative.[47] For some critical realists the use of quantitative methods is more controversial than qualitative methods.[48]

Standard econometrics focuses on identifying regular outcomes and treats variables of interest as separable and additive isolates, which in turn either assumes highly stable conditions (in the 'data generating process') or applies treatments to the data to make it sufficiently well-behaved.[49] For critics this only works well in closed system situations and because of this some argue that descriptive statistics are usually preferable to analytical statistics.[50] However, there are many realists and many heterodox economists (who are not critical realists) who argue that the bigger problem is a presumption of use of quantitative methods (so too much of the field is devoted to them at the expense of other approaches) and insufficient understanding of their limits. Stable institutions and routines can lead to relatively regular outcomes and for some this provides an argument for careful use of analytical statistics in combination with other methods.[51] There are also many quantitative methods that do not rely on either linear functions or stable frequency table-based probability and there are various

[46] Note: most sports economists are likely to be familiar with modelling so there seems little point providing a detailed reference to either hypothesis testing or different econometric techniques and tests.

[47] For discussion, see Max (2008), Johnson et al. (2007).

[48] Note, Tony Lawson, for example, is a well-known sceptic regarding mathematical modelling and use of econometrics. Doug Porpora (2001) and Petter Næss (2004) are well-known advocates of the limited use of models and regression.

[49] For detailed discussion of econometrics research for sports economics, see Chap. 12 'Econometric models in sports economics' (Leeds & McCormick, 2017/2006) in *Handbook of Sports Economics Research*.

[50] Note, for example, among well-known critical realists, besides Tony Lawson, Andrew Sayer and Steve Fleetwood are known to hold this view.

[51] Many heterodox economists, most of whom are post Keynesians, make this argument and several of the contributions to the Downward edited handbook take this approach. Mark Setterfield, for example, adopts an 'open system ceteris paribus' (OSCP) approach (see Setterfield, 2003, 2016). Sheila Dow's position might best be described as 'sitting on the fence' (e.g. Dow, 2003). She often draws on Lawson's arguments on methodology (often pointing out similarities to the thinking of John Maynard Keynes) but also draws on the work of well-known post Keynesian modellers, including her long-time collaborator Victoria Chick, who sadly recently died. See also Murray Glickman who argues we can interpret statistical findings as indicative or traces of causal mechanisms and of tendencies using retroduction (Glickman, 2003).

critical realists who advocate these and critics of critical realism who argue that realists should do more to adopt them.[52]

In any case, it is not my purpose in this chapter to argue against the use of methods but rather to highlight the great range of possible methods sports economists might use in a research strategy, while placing emphasis on the need to justify their use. To be clear, there is plenty of work across the social sciences using and combining the methods I have mentioned. This does not make my argument superfluous and I am not trying to 'reinvent the wheel'; the positive purpose of this section is to encourage sports economists to make best use of what is available and perhaps to be more ambitious and open-minded. Of course, no researcher's skillset can make them aware of or expert in every method and this implies a need for economists to be more interdisciplinary (by which I don't mean occupying the space of other disciplines and imposing the economist's toolkit—this leads to economics imperialism as well as very limited relations to other disciplines and their practitioners). The well-known critical realist Berth Danermark has written a great deal about this (he is an expert in the study of disability and prior to retirement managed a centre for interdisciplinary research on this subject in Sweden for decades). According to Danermark, effective interdisciplinarity highlights the need for critical dialogue regarding ontology because without this there is a high risk that collaboration degenerates into misunderstanding and eclectic and incompatible work.[53] Discussion of ontology (the questions this raises that we have discussed throughout) provides an important focus for justification of work. But as Danermark makes clear, this is only a step towards judgement regarding any particular study or finding and this brings me finally to triangulation.

Triangulation is not solely a realist concept—as Denzin notes, its history can be traced through at least three 'paradigm wars' over 50 years (Denzin, 2010). It is, however, now closely associated with retroduction (and abduction), and one of the best-known advocates of triangulation is Wendy Olsen, a critical realist development economist, well-known for her work on both the methodology and application of multiple and mixed

[52] While Wendy Olsen makes a case for econometrics, she also makes an argument for case-based quantitative methods which do not rely on frequency based probability and this is a perspective she shares with Dave Byrne (2002). For an example of researchers who criticise critical realism for its lack of development of innovative quantitative methods, see also Williams and Dyer (2004).

[53] See Danermark (2019) and the interview, Danermark and Morgan (2023).

methods.[54] According to Olsen, triangulation involves bringing together disparate parts of a research strategy in terms of guiding questions to interrogate use of different methods and compare their findings, but also encourages iterative exploration of findings and questions (and this may also mean going back to any subjects in qualitative components of work and reinterpreting any quantitative results):

> Triangulation is the combination of methods or techniques. [The metaphor draws on its use for location] In gathering data to make maps, three or more high-level vantage points are used to start building up a picture of the land lying in the low area between them. Measures of the angles from each vantage point to each thing in the space enable us to re-confirm the relative location of each thing in the space. The word triangulation also suggests the possibility that the view from each vantage point may be different. From one point, some items in the landscape may be masked (as in survey research when the respondent is nearly silenced). From another point, clouds move in and mask the view (as in structured interviewing if the researcher sticks too closely to an a priori theoretical or discursive framework). And from a third viewpoint, one might get a clear view of the first two viewpoints, and of the measuring instruments at those viewpoints. Triangulation may enable better measurement, but it will also reveal differences of interpretation and meaning [and this applies also to quantitative methods and findings]. (Olsen, 2003, p. 159)

It seems likely that the way many economists are currently socialised, trained and encouraged to focus down on analytical statistical tests will mean they find triangulation unsatisfactory and unsettling. Triangulation offers no clear-cut answers and implies there is no decisive test.

In the main canon of sports economics, use of mixed methods is rare, although one is able to see its application in other sports contexts. For example, De Bosscher et al. (2010) apply mixed methods to the comparison of elite sports systems in the *Journal of Sport Management*. In the *Sport Management Review*, Rudd and Burke Johnson (2010) called for more mixed methods in sport management research. More recently, Guest and Luijten (2018), in the journal *Sport in Society*, examine fan culture and attendance in women's football using mixed methods and a triangulated analysis, combining ethnographic observation and interview. I would

---

[54] Note: in terms of the history of ideas, mixed methods and triangulation are often associated with American pragmatism.

point out though that triangulation follows from multiple and mixed methods and these are uncontroversial outside of economics. Not only are there many research methods texts which advocate multiple and mixed methods, many professional bodies and institutes endorse them.[55] From this point of view, it is economics that is, despite its 'empirical turn' (which one should acknowledge has diversified quantitative methods and improved the use of experiment and simulation), out of step. It is economics on the dominant side of the divide that should feel the pressure to justify itself rather than the reverse.[56]

CONCLUSION: A TURN IN SPORTS ECONOMICS?

In this chapter I have essentially made an argument for a 'turn' in sports economics. The argument is made thematically and cumulatively in a series of sections. With the idea in mind of a divide in economics and the need to reassess economics from the other side of this divide, I first go back to basics and provide an introduction to critical realism. This turns on the concepts of ontological realism, epistemological relativism and judgemental rationality. The argument for an open systems non-atomistic agent-structure framework is made within the context of these concepts. I then turn to behavioural economics and especially the work of Daniel Kahneman. I first set out some key aspects of the approach to an agent associated with behavioural economics and then establish that there is more diversity in the theory and concepts of behavioural economics than

[55] Denzin, for example, mentions among others in the US, the American Educational Research Association, the American Statistical Association, the Institute of Educational Sciences, the National Institute of Health, the National Research Council and the National Science Foundation (Denzin, 2010, p. 419). For a discussion of mixed methods in sports research (not economics), see Gibson (2019).

[56] Note, I have not mentioned Lawson's work on demi-regularity and contrast explanation (see, e.g. Lawson, 2003). Demi-regularity is not necessarily the same as relative stability of institutions leading to relative stability of events, since Lawson argues different mixes of causal mechanisms can still lead to stable outcomes for some period. Downward and Mearman (2003), however, draw on demi-regularity to develop a mixed methods research strategy. Contrast explanation is concerned with initiating research through the identification of either unexpected enduring patterns or the sudden breakdown of patterns (both can be contrasts since the contrast is with what is expected). In a later paper they return to the subject of retroduction, triangulation and mixed methods, see Downward and Mearman (2007). Lawson provides a discussion of the use of triangulation in economics in one of his replies to 'critics' published in Fullbrook (2009). See Lawson (2009).

one might think. This provides an opportunity to rethink the agent and I make the case that Kahneman's work can be repositioned on the other side of the divide and do so with reference to critical realism—hence 'hybrid'. I illustrate this with work from *Thinking Fast and Slow*, and especially System 1 and System 2 thinking insofar as these draw attention to the sociality of the psychology of the agent. Finally, I turn to the development of a research strategy for sports attendance demand compatible with the argument I have made. Rather than deduction or induction this begins from retroduction and I then elaborate a series of possible lines of inquiry one might follow in sports attendance demand. In the last section I place this strategy within multi and mixed methods and suggest that the challenges this introduces suggest a need for interdisciplinarity and for some way to iteratively develop and make compatible diverse research and findings. I point out that there is a long tradition of this and the main term used is triangulation.

The takeaway from this chapter—which as I stated in the introduction is only a 'sketch'—is that sports attendance demand can be very different than economists currently make it. Some might argue that the actual message is that economics should be sociology or some other social science, but this would be to miss the point. Implicit to my argument is that since the object of study is the same as sociology of sport, etc., it would be a sign of progress that economics became more compatible with these and more open to dialogue based on common understandings. This is surely served by some common concepts (e.g. an agent-structure framework), greater diversity of methods and a more flexible methodological approach. However, many sociologists might read this and wonder what the fuss is about, since they do much of what I advocate here already (and it should also be noted some have adopted aspects from economics).[57] This too would miss the point, since arguably as things stand few other social scientists would be able to follow the technical aspects of economic research on sports attendance and might find themselves mystified by much of its

---

[57] See, for example, the typical subject matter in sociology of sport, culture of sport and sports psychology journals (much of this is about participation rather than support and attendance, but the methods and concepts still apply). Well-known journals include: *Sport in Society—Cultures, Commerce, Media, Politics*, *European Journal of Sport and Society*, *Sociology of Sport Journal*, *International Review for the Sociology of Sport*, *Leisure Studies*, *The Sport Psychologist*. For further discussion of overlap with sociology in economics, see the references in the discussion earlier in the paper regarding diversity and progress in behavioural economics, especially Ross (2023).

starting point focused on the standard agent. Dialogue requires the possibility of what philosophers term 'commensuration'. There are many economists who make the case for greater pluralism in economics and Sheila Dow is notable for making this kind of argument (e.g. Dow, 2012b, 2012c). This does not mean, however, 'you do your thing, I do mine and we ignore each other or tolerate each other' and it doesn't mean 'anything goes'. Rather, 'structured pluralism' means an attitude to learning and open-minded dialogue. For this to occur, perhaps sports economics needs a 'gestalt switch' and I hope this chapter plays some small part in encouraging such a switch.

REFERENCES

Altman, H., Altman, M., & Torgler, B. (Eds.). (2022). *Behavioural sports economics: A research companion*. Routledge.

Altman, M. (2004). The nobel prize in behavioral and experimental economics: A contextual and critical appraisal of the contributions of Daniel Kahneman and Vernon Smith. *Review of Political Economy, 16*(1), 3–41.

Angner, E. (2012). *A course in behavioral economics*. Palgrave Macmillan.

Angner, E. (2015). To navigate safely in the vast sea of empirical facts: Ontology and methodology in behavioral economics. *Synthese, 192*(11), 3557–3575.

Angner, E. (2019). We're all behavioral economists now. *Journal of Economic Methodology, 26*(3), 195–207.

Archer, M. S. (1995). *Realist social theory: The morphogenetic approach*. Cambridge University Press.

Atkinson, M. (2016). Ethnography. In B. Smith & A. C. Sparkes (Eds.), *(2019). Routledge handbook of qualitative research in sports and exercise* (pp. 49–61). Routledge.

Avtonomov, V., & Avtonomov, Y. (2019). Four Methodenstreits between behavioral and mainstream economics. *Journal of Economic Methodology, 26*(3), 179–194.

Bell, E., Harley, B., & Bryman, A. (2022). *Business research methods* (5th ed.). Oxford University Press.

Bhaskar, R. (1979). *The possibility of naturalism*. Harvester.

Bhaskar, R., & Lawson, T. (1998). Introduction: Basic texts and developments. In M. S. Archer, R. Bhaskar, A. Collier, T. Lawson, & A. Norrie (Eds.), *Critical realism: Essential readings* (pp. 3–15). Routledge.

Bond, A. J., Cockayne, D., Ludvigsen, J. A. L., Maguire, K., Parnell, D., Plumley, D., Widdop, P., & Wilson, R. (2022). COVID-19: The return of football fans. *Managing Sport and Leisure, 27*(1–2), 102–112.

Braesemann, F. (2019). How behavioural economics relates to psychology—Some bibliographic evidence. *Journal of Economic Methodology, 26*(2), 133–146.

Buch-Hansen, H., & Nielsen, P. (2020). *Critical realism: Basics and beyond.* Red Globe Press.

Byrne, D. (2002). *Interpreting quantitative data.* Sage.

Collier, A. (1994). *Critical realism.* Verso.

Danermark, B. (2019). Applied interdisciplinary research—A critical realist perspective. *Journal of Critical Realism, 18*(4), 368–382.

Danermark, B., & Morgan, J. (2023). Applying critical realism in an interdisciplinary context: An interview with Berth Danermark. *Journal of Critical Realism, 22*(3), 525–561.

De Bosscher, V., Shibli, S., Van Bottenburg, M., De Knop, P., & Truyens, J. (2010). Developing a method for comparing the elite sport systems and policies of nations: A mixed research methods approach. *Journal of Sport Management, 24*(5), 567–600.

Denzin, N. (2010). Moments, mixed methods, and paradigm dialogs. *Qualitative Inquiry, 16*(6), 419–427.

Dick, B. (2005). Conflict and cooperation: Institutional and behavioral economics. *Journal of Economic Issues, 39*(3), 819–820.

Dow, S. (2003). Critical realism and economics. In P. Downward (Ed.), *Applied economics and the critical realist critique* (pp. 12–26). Routledge.

Dow, S. (2012a). The issue of uncertainty in economics. In S. Dow (Ed.), *Foundations for new economic thinking: A collection of essays* (pp. 197–209). Palgrave Macmillan.

Dow, S. (2012b). Beyond dualism. In S. Dow (Ed.), *Foundations for new economic thinking: A collection of essays* (pp. 52–71). Palgrave Macmillan.

Dow, S. (2012c). Structured pluralism. In S. Dow (Ed.), *Foundations for new economic thinking: A collection of essays* (pp. 162–177). Palgrave Macmillan.

Downward, P., Dawson, A., & Dejonghe, E. (2009). *Sports economics: Theory, evidence and policy.* Routledge.

Downward, P., Frick, B., Humphreys, B., Pawlowski, T., Ruseski, J., & Soebbing, B. (Eds.). (2019). *The sage handbook of sports economics.* Sage.

Downward, P., & Mearman, A. (2003). Critical realism and econometrics: Interaction between philosophy and post-Keynesian practice. In P. Downward (Ed.), *Applied economics and the critical realist critique* (pp. 111–128). Routledge.

Downward, P., & Mearman, A. (2007). Retroduction as mixed-methods triangulation in economic research: Reorienting economics into social science. *Cambridge Journal of Economics, 31*(1), 77–99.

Earl, P. E. (2018). Richard H. Thaler: A Nobel prize for behavioural economics. *Review of Political Economy, 30*(2), 107–125.

Edwards, P., O'Mahoney, J., & Vincent, S. (Eds.). (2014). *Studying organizations using critical realism: A practical guide.* Oxford University Press.

Elder-Vass, D. (2012). *The reality of social construction.* Routledge.

Fizel, J. (Ed.). (2017/2006). *Handbook of sports economic research.* Routledge.

Fleetwood, S. (Ed.). (1999). *Critical realism in economics.* Routledge.

Frerichs, S. (2019). Bounded sociality: Behavioural economists' truncated understanding of the social and its implications for politics. *Journal of Economic Methodology, 26*(3), 243–258.

Fullbrook, E. (Ed.). (2009). *Ontology and economics.* Routledge.

Gibson, K. (2019). Mixed methods research in sports and exercise: Integrating qualitative research. In B. Smith & A. C. Sparkes (Eds.), *Routledge handbook of qualitative research in sports and exercise* (pp. 382–396). Routledge.

Glickman, M. (2003). From predictive to indicative statistics: Explaining corporate borrowing. In P. Downward (Ed.), *Applied economics and the critical realist critique* (pp. 247–265). Routledge.

Groff, R. (2004). *Critical realism, post-positivism and the possibility of knowledge.* Routledge.

Guest, A., & Luijten, A. (2018). Fan culture and motivation in the context of successful women's professional team sports: A mixed-methods case study of Portland Thorns fandom. *Sport in Society, 21*(7), 1013–1030.

Hartwig, M. (Ed.). (2007). *Dictionary of critical realism.* Routledge.

Heukelom, F. (2014a). *Behavioural economics: A history.* Cambridge University Press.

Heukelom, F. (2014b). Mainstreaming behavioral economics. *Journal of Economic Methodology, 21*(1), 92–95.

Hodgson, G. (2019). *Is there a future for heterodox economics?* Edward Elgar.

Hopcraft, A. (2013/1968). *The football man: People and passions in soccer.* Aurum.

Jessop, B. (2005). Critical realism and the strategic-relational approach. *New Formations, 56,* 40–53.

Johnson, R. B., Onmegbuzie, A. J., & Turner, L. A. (2007). Towards a definition of mixed methods research. *Journal of Mixed Methods Research, 1*(2), 112–133.

Kahneman, D. (1991). Article commentary: Judgment and decision making: A personal view. *Psychological Science, 2*(3), 142–145.

Kahneman, D. (2002) Biographical. The Sveriges Riksbank prize in economic sciences in memory of Alfred Nobel 2002. https://www.nobelprize.org/prizes/economic-sciences/2002/kahneman/biographical/

Kahneman, D. (2011). *Thinking fast and slow.* Penguin.

Kahneman, D., & Tversky, A. (1979). Prospect theory: An analysis of decision under risk. *Econometrica, 47*(2), 263–292.

Kahneman, D., & Tversky, A. (Eds.). (2000). *Choices, values, and frames.* Cambridge University Press.

Karni, E. (2016). Savage's subjective expected utility model. In M. Vernengo, E. Caldentey, & B. Rosser Jr. (Eds.), *The new Palgrave dictionary of economics.* Palgrave Macmillan. Online continuously updating version. https://doi.org/1 0.1057/978-1-349-95121-5_2467-1

Lawson, T. (1997). *Economics and reality.* Routledge.

Lawson, T. (2003). *Reorienting economics.* Routledge.

Lawson, T. (2009). Triangulation and social research: Reply to Downward and Mearman. In E. Fullbrook (Ed.), *Ontology and economics: Tony Lawson and his critics* (pp. 142–157). Routledge.

Lawson, T. (2019). *The nature of social reality.* Routledge.

Lecouteux, G. (2023). The Homer Economicus narrative: From cognitive psychology to individual public policies. *Journal of Economic Methodology, 30*(2), 176–187.

Lee, H. L. (2009). The impact of postseason restructuring on the competitive balance and fan demand in Major League Baseball. *Journal of Sports Economics, 10*(3), 219–235.

Leeds, M., & McCormick, B. (2017/2006). Econometric models in sports economics. In J. Fizel (Ed.), *Handbook of sports economic research* (pp. 221–236). Routledge.

Lewis, P. (Ed.). (2004). *Transforming economics: Perspectives on the critical realist project.* Routledge.

Machina, M. J. (2008). Expected utility hypothesis. In S. N. Durlauf & L. E. Blume (Eds.), *The new Palgrave dictionary of economics* (2nd ed.). Palgrave Macmillan.

Max, B. M. (Ed.). (2008). *Advances in mixed methods research.* Sage.

Mongin, P. (1997). Expected utility theory. In J. Davis, D. W. Hands, & U. Mäki (Eds.), *Handbook of economic methodology* (pp. 342–350). Edward Elgar.

Morgan, J. (2016a). Critical realism as a social ontology for economics. In S. Lee & B. Cronin (Eds.), *Handbook of research methods and applications in heterodox economics* (pp. 15–34). Edward Elgar.

Morgan, J. (Ed.). (2016b). *What is neoclassical economics?* Routledge.

Morgan, J., & Embery, J. (2018). Heterodox economics as a living body of knowledge: Community, (in)commensurability, critical engagement and pluralism. In T. H. Jo, L. Chester, & C. D'Ippoliti (Eds.), *The Routledge handbook of heterodox economics* (pp. 515–533). Routledge.

Næss, P. (2004). Prediction, regressions and critical realism. *Journal of Critical Realism, 3*(1), 133–164.

Olsen, W. (2003). Triangulation, time and the social objects of econometrics. In P. Downward (Ed.), *Applied economics and the critical realist critique* (pp. 153–169). Routledge.

Parnell, D., Rookwood, J., Bond, A., Widdop, P., & Ludvigsen, J. A. L. (2022). 'It's a whole new ball game': Thirty years of the English premier league. *Soccer and Society, 23*(4–5), 329–333.

Porpora, D. V. (2001). Do realists run regressions? In J. Lopez & G. Potter (Eds.), *After postmodernism: An introduction to critical realism* (pp. 260–266). Athlone Press.

Power, M. J., Widdop, P., Parnell, D., Carr, J., & Millar, S. R. (2020). Football and politics: The politics of football. *Managing Sport and Leisure, 25*(1–2), 1–5.

Pratten, S. (Ed.). (2015). *Social ontology in modern economics.* Routledge.

Ross, D. (2023). Economics is converging with sociology but not with psychology. *Journal of Economic Methodology, 30*(2), 135–156.

Rudd, A., & Burke Johnson, R. (2010). A call for more mixed methods in sports management research. *Sport Management Review, 13*(1), 14–24.

Savage, L. J. (1954). *The foundations of statistics.* New York: John Wiley and Sons.

Sayer, A. (1992). *Method in social science* (2nd ed.). Routledge.

Sayer, A. (2011). *Why things matter to people: Social science, values and ethical life.* Cambridge University Press.

Sayer, A., & Morgan, J. (2022). A realist journey through social theory and political economy: An interview with Andrew Sayer. *Journal of Critical Realism, 21*(4), 434–470.

Schreyer, D. (2022). Moving towards behavioural stadium attendance demand research: First lessons learned from exploring football spectator no-show behaviour in Europe. In H. Altman, M. Altman, & B. Torgler (Eds.), *Behavioural sports economics: A research companion* (pp. 264–286). Routledge.

Schumpeter, J. (1997/1954). *History of economic analysis.* Routledge.

Setterfield, M. (2003). Critical realism and formal modelling: incompatible bedfellows? In P. Downward (Ed.), *Applied economics and the critical realist critique* (pp. 71–88). Routledge.

Setterfield, M. (2016). Heterodox economics, social ontology and the use of mathematics. In J. Morgan (Ed.), *What is neoclassical economics?* (pp. 221–237). Routledge.

Simon, H. (1987). Bounded rationality. In J. Eatwell, M. Milgate, & P. Newman (Eds.), *The new Palgrave: A dictionary of economics* (Vol. 1, pp. 266–268). Macmillan.

Singal, J. (2013). Interview: Daniel Kahneman's gripe with behavioral economics. *Daily Beast,* 26th April. https://www.thedailybeast.com/daniel-kahnemans-gripe-with-behavioral-economics

Smith, B., & Sparkes, A. C. (Eds.). (2019). *Routledge handbook of qualitative research in sports and exercise.* Routledge.

Stanfield, K. C. (2023). Evolutionary behavioral economics: Veblenian institutionalist insights from recent evidence. *Journal of Economic Issues, 57*(3), 693–710.

Tversky, A., & Kahneman, D. (1974). Judgment under uncertainty: Heuristics and biases: Biases in judgments reveal some heuristics of thinking under uncertainty. *Science, 185*(4157), 1124–1131.

Williams, M., & Dyer, W. (2004). Realism and probability. In B. Carter & C. New (Eds.), *Making realism work: Realist social theory and empirical research* (pp. 67–85). Routledge.

Yilmaz, O., Easley, R. F., & Ferguson, M. E. (2023). The future of sports ticketing: Technologies, data and new strategies. *Journal of Revenue Pricing Management, 22*(3), 219–230.

CHAPTER 5

Afterword: Ways Forward

Abstract In this final comment, I highlight some of the potential methodological applications that follow organically from the wide-ranging discussion in the previous chapters. The comments and suggestions highlight thematic possibilities. In particular, I comment on the scope for retroduction and also the potential to pursue existing conceptual and empirical concerns of economists in regard of attendance demand, albeit in a changed context.

Keywords Attendance demand • Methodology • Retroduction

It would have been relatively easy to take the conventional route an economist might take in studying attendance demand: collect some data, develop a model with a focus on variables of interest and run some regressions. This, however, could never achieve what it is I set out to do and the whole point was not to take this approach. Given the dominance of this way of approaching the subject matter, it made good sense to focus on methodology. However, there are many ways one might add substance to the general methodological claims and research strategy I have set out in the three previous chapters.

J. Embery, *Attendance Demand in Sports Economics*, Palgrave Pivots in Sports Economics, https://doi.org/10.1007/978-3-031-60040-1_5

Clearly, if one's subject matter is attendance demand, the main metrics (the core data) remain the same as those for any other researcher in sports economics, including what I referred to as the dominant side of the divide. The numbers attending are simply the numbers attending, and what somebody pays to attend a team sports event is simply what somebody pays. The decision to do so, and the experiences had, exist irrespective of whether anyone researches them (though one cannot discount the 'performative' influence that published research can have on attitudes that influence behaviour, since beliefs and reasons affect what we do). However, a research strategy that follows on from *what I have argued* will provide very different explanations than found in much of current sports economics research.

Wendy Olsen in her book *Data Collection* provides a useful set of questions one can apply in interrogating data. This provides a useful reminder to economists that data has context and is more than its patterns and quantities. She associates this with 'retroduction':

1. What caused the original data to show the patterns it showed? This question includes: why did I start off with the topic that I had set up in the beginning? Were there theoretical reasons? If so, were they good ones, or does the theory have some problems? Or were there ethical reasons, and if so what else do I need to know about in order to develop a strong ethical argument about the topic?

2. What causes unique, unusual, deviant or inexplicable cases to turn out as they do? Here it may initially seem that speculation is needed. But scientific speculation is also a more formal type of logic which is more like discernment. We have to ask (a) is it possible that the usual theories can explain the unusual, and if so why was it hidden from us at first? And (b) if the usual theories do not explain the unusual, then what could? What kind of new theory do I need? What new addition to the lexicon would help me in discerning either meanings, explanations or an overall interpretation that helps make sense of these unusual cases?

3. What are the complex standpoints and viewpoints that are behind the contradictory results in this research? Or in other words, what are the sources of tension, and what have we learned that was not already known about these tensions? How do other people interpret the same data (or events)? Why are their interpretations different from the researchers' findings? (Olsen, 2012, pp. 215–216)

'Interpretation' and iterative critique of theory play little formal role in economics at the moment. In terms of attendance demand, currently socialisation and enculturation are undertheorised and under-researched. It seems that there is a far greater role for qualitative research. Based on this research there will likely be a whole set of associated evidence that can shed light on the available metrics or data that economists typically work with. Any findings will likely be more granular and diverse. While this may be problematic from one point of view for economists, since it adds a different kind of complexity to their work, it does also hold out the prospect of a different kind of practical significance for the work of economists. Economists should not fear this prospect but rather see it as an opportunity (if we accept mixed methods as a standard).

REFERENCE

Olsen, W. (2012). *Data collection: Key debates and methods in social research.* Sage.

Appendices

APPENDIX A: TABULATED BREAKDOWN OF KEY CONTENTS OF THE MAIN DEDICATED SPORT ECONOMICS TEXTBOOKS[1]

Author(S)	Title, edition, publisher	Year of publication	Contains initial 'toolkit' chapter (thinking like an economist, presupposing mainstream framework)	Develops 'key concepts'—standard series of chapters focussing on demand and supply conditions, theory of markets (product, labour), peculiarity of sports within the framework	Presupposes or discusses the 'standard agent'	Provides additional chapter(s) discussing 'alternative'/theories/approaches
Downward, P. and Dawson, A.	The Economics of Professional Team Sports, 1st Ed., Routledge	2000	✓	✓	x	✓
Gratton, C. and Taylor, P.	The Economics of Sport and Recreation: An Economic Analysis, 1st Ed., Routledge	2000	✓	✓	✓	x
Sandy, R., Sloane, P. and Rosentraub, M.	The Economics of Sport—An International Perspective, 1st Ed., Palgrave Macmillan	2006	✓	✓	✓	x
Downward, P., Dawson, A. and Dejonghe, T.	Sports Economics—Theory, Evidence and Policy, 1st Ed., Routledge	2009	✓	✓	✓	x

Author	Title	Year				
Fort, R.	*Sports Economics*, 3rd Ed. Pearson	2010	✓	✓	✓	X
Blair, R. D.	*Sports Economics*, 1st Ed, Cambridge University Press	2012	✓	✓	✓	X
Kesenne, S.	*The Economic Theory of Professional Team Sports*, 1st Ed., Edward Elgar	2014	✓	✓	✓	X
Humphreys, B.	*Economics of Professional Sports*, 1st Ed., BRH Publishing	2015	✓	✓	✓	X
Berri, D.	*Sports Economics*, 1st Ed, Worth Publishers	2019	✓	✓	X	✓
Leeds, M., Von Allmen, P. and Matheson, V. A.	*Sports Economics*, 7th Ed., Routledge	2023	✓	✓	✓	X

[1] Note: there are other textbooks dealing with sports management, leisure management and sports finance, as well as collected essays. Cursory reading of titles may cause some confusion. The textbooks here provide an interesting supporting source for some of the survey claims made in my first paper.

APPENDIX B: USEFUL SUPPORTING QUOTES

'Where an experiment has been so set up that one mechanism alone operates, we have a closed system. In fact, no system in our Universe is ever perfectly closed, but experiments can approximate close enough to closure for the purposes of science. It is a characteristic of closed systems that in them a given causal stimulus will always produce the same effect: experiments are repeatable ... an experiment may make them [mechanisms] operate when they were not operating before, but that is not the same as making them come into being where they did not exist before, otherwise the experiment would be no discovery, but an invention. Hence, things have unexercised powers, and powers that are unexercised unrealised and powers that are realised unperceived' (Collier, 1994, pp. 33 and 36–37).

'Things have the powers that they do because of their structures then, we can investigate the structures that generate the powers ... In asking about the structure generating some power of some entity, we are asking about a *mechanism* generating an *event* ... In open systems, a multiplicity of mechanisms is operating, conjointly bringing about a series of events, ... The series of events that occurs can be called the Actual ... but the mechanisms that codetermine it are just as *real* not ... not all events are experienced ... when we find the garden muddy in the morning we assume a real rainstorm, though we slept through it; a murder victim implies a murderer, even though one may never be identified' (Collier, 1994, pp. 43–44).

'*Strata* ... mechanisms are, so to speak, *layers* of nature, and are *ordered*, not just jumbled up together, ... animals do not break the laws of physics and chemistry. They are after all composed of atoms, and those atoms obey the same laws whether or not they are parts of living organisms. So animals are necessarily governed by *both* kinds of law, physico-chemical and biological. Minerals, while not *governed* by biological laws, are nevertheless *affected* by them ... In discussing the stratification of nature, one must keep it in mind that it is *mechanisms*, not things or events that are stratified. As Bhaskar puts it: the predicates "natural", "social", "human", "physical", "chemical", "aerodynamical", "biological", "economic", etc ought not to be regarded as differentiating distinct kind of events, but as differentiating distinct kinds of *mechanisms*' (Collier, 1994, pp. 46–47).

'No social theory can be advanced without making some assumptions about what kind of reality it is dealing with and how to explain it. All social theory is ontologically shaped and methodologically moulded even if these processes remain covert and scarcely acknowledged by the practitioner. This is inescapable because theories logically entail concepts and concepts themselves include certain things and exclude others (at the methodological level) and denote some aspects of reality whilst denying others (at the ontological level). Any who thinks they can avoid both fall into the trap of instrumentalism: those believing that the use of 'heuristic concepts' in explanation saves them from making any ontological commitment fail to recognise that terming something 'heuristic' is itself a matter of ontology' (Archer, 1995, pp. 57–58).

'Social structure, which is conceived of by Methodological Realists as [only] 'systems of human relations among social positions is rejected primarily because structures refer to actual forms of social organisation, that is, to real entities with their own powers, tendencies and potentials, secondly, because the social relations upon which they depend are held to have independent causal properties rather than being mere abstractions from our repetitive and routinised behaviour and, most importantly, because these relations which constitute structures predate occupants of positions within them, thus constraining or enabling agency, in short, realists, who would also disassociate themselves from the definitions endorsed by Individualists and Holists, see social *structure as quintessentially relational* but none the less real because of its emergent properties which affect the agents who act within it and thus cannot be reduced to their activities' (Archer, 1995, p. 106).

'I would argue that the most important aspect of "agency" is the capacity to "make a difference" to society, but do not see that this necessarily entails activity *especially* if this means an ability "to have done otherwise" [since in some cases simply being or having a presence e.g. demographic composition of society affects society]' (Archer, 1995, pp. 118–119).

'The concept of emergence is essential to our understanding of these structures and theory causal powers because it enable us to see how the entities at each level can have causal powers of their own, despite being in a sense "nothing more" than a collection of lower level parts. Relational emergence theory argues that entities may possess emergence properties, that are produced by mechanisms that in turn depends on the property's of the entities parts and how these parts are organised' (Elder-Vass, 2010, p. 192).

'Rather than starting with a question about an aspect of social reality and determining an appropriate method, modern economists usually start with a particular type of method and presume mistakenly, that it must be appropriate to all social contexts' (Lawson, 2015a, 2015b, p. 13).

'[I]t can be seen that reliance on the sorts of mathematical modelling methods adopted by economists presupposes a ubiquity of correlations or regularities of the form "whenever X then Y", where X and Y are outcomes of measurable "variables" of some sort (events, states of affairs, etc.). Of course, the number of types of outcomes or "variables" involved can be few or many, and the nature of the correlations simple or complex, linear or non-linear, deterministic or stochastic, a priori, empirical or simulated, and so on. I focus here on the basic form. Systems that support such correlations, I have already noted, can be called closed, and the dependency of explanatory endeavour on such closures renders the modelling exercises a form of deductivism … if the correlations are to be supported by systematic theorising, then theoretical entities posited in accompanying analyses are necessarily constrained to take the forms of isolated atoms. They are atomistic in the sense that, for each one, where any specified conditions X are repeated the entity must, on each occasion, react in the same predictable way, Y say. And each atom must be considered as acting in isolation to ensure that in the context of the model nothing interacts with the atom's operation preventing its effect Y (given X) from being actualised or occurring. Thus, the doll will (predictably) walk forward (Y) each time it is wound up and placed on the table (X), if it is isolated from the effects of the wind or a passing dog etc.' (Lawson, 2021, p. 43) (Tables B.1 and B.2).

Victoria Chick and Sheila Dow's useful tabulation of their version of Open systems and Closed systems.

'By uncertain knowledge, let me explain, I do not mean to merely distinguish what is known or certain from what is only probable. The game of roulette is not subject, in this sense, to uncertainty; … Even the weather is only moderately uncertain. The sense in which I am using the term is that in which the prospect of a European war is uncertain, or the price of copper and the rate of interest twenty years hence, or the obsolescence of the new invention, or the position of private wealth owners in the social system in 1970. About these matters there is not scientific basis on which to form any calculable probability whatever. We simply do not know' (Keynes, 1937, pp. 213–214).

Table B.1   Conditions for open systems

Real-world systems
- The system is not atomistic; therefore at least one of the following holds:
  - Outcomes of actions cannot be inferred from individual actions (because of interactions);
  - Agents and their interactions may change (for example agents may learn).
- Structure and agency are interdependent.
- Boundaries around and within the social and economic system are mutable; for at least one of the following reasons:
  - Social structures may evolve;
  - Connections between structures may change;
  - The structure-agent relation may change.
- Identifiable social structures are embedded in larger social structures; these may mutually interact, for the boundaries of a social system are in general partial or semi-permeable.

Implications for theoretical systems
- There may be important omitted variables or relations and/or their effects on the system may be uncertain.
- The classification into exogenous and endogenous variables may be neither fixed nor exhaustive.
- Connections and/or boundaries between structures may be imperfectly known and/or may change.
- There is imperfect knowledge of the relations between variables; relationships may not be stable.

Table B.2   Conditions for close theoretical systems

- All relevant variables can be identified.
- The boundaries of the system are definite and immutable; it follows that it is clear which variables are exogenous and which are endogenous; these categories are fixed.
- Only the specified exogenous variables affect the system, and they do this in a known way.
- Relations between the included variables are either knowable or random.
- Economic agents (whether individuals or aggregates) are treated atomistically.
- The nature of the economic agents is treated as if constant.
- The structure of the relationships between the components (variables, subsystems, agents) is treated as if it is either knowable or random.
- The structural framework within which agents act is taken as given.

(Chick & Dow, 2005, pp. 366–367)

References

Altman, M. (2017). A bounded rationality assessment of the new behavioural economics. In R. Frantz, S. Chen, K. Dopfer, F. Heukelom, & S. Mousavi (Eds.), *Routledge handbook of behavioural economics* (pp. 179–193). Routledge.

Archer, M. S. (1995). *Realist social theory: The morphogenetic approach*. Cambridge University Press.

Archer, M. S., Bhaskar, R., Collier, A., Lawson, T., & Norrie, A. (Eds.). (1998). *Critical realism: Essential readings*. Routledge.

Baimbridge, M., Cameron, S., & Dawson, P. (1996). Satellite television and demand for football: A whole new ball game? *Scottish Journal of Political Economy, 43*(3), 317–333.

Berri, D. (2019). *Sports economics*. Worth Publishers.

Blair, R. D. (2012). *Sports economics*. Cambridge University Press.

Chick, V., & Dow, S. (2005). The meaning of open systems. *Journal of Economic Methodology, 12*(3), 363–381.

Collier, A. (1994). *Critical realism*. Verso.

Downward, P., & Dawson, A. (2000). *The economics of professional team sports*. Routledge.

Edwards, W. (1954). The theory of decision making. *Psychological Bulletin, 51*(4), 380–417.

Elder-Vass, D. (2010). *The causal power of social structures: Emergence structure and agency*. Cambridge University Press.

Fort, R. (2011). *Sports economics* (3rd ed.). Upper Saddle River, NJ.

© The Author(s), under exclusive license to Springer Nature Switzerland AG 2024
J. Embery, *Attendance Demand in Sports Economics*, Palgrave Pivots in Sports Economics,
https://doi.org/10.1007/978-3-031-60040-1

Friedman, M. (1953). The methodology of positive economics. In *Essays in positive economics*. University of Chicago Press.

Funk, D. C., Filo, K., Beaton, A. A., & Pritchard, M. (2009). Measuring the motives of sport event attendance: Bridging the academic- practitioner divide to understanding behaviour. *Sport Marketing Quarterly, 18*(3), 126–138.

Gratton, C., & Taylor, P. (2000). *The economics of sport and recreation: An economic analysis*. Routledge.

Humphreys, B. (2015). *Economics of professional sports*. BRH Publishing.

Kesenne, S. (2000). Revenue sharing and competitive in professional team sports. *Journal of Sports Economics, 1*(1), 56–65.

Kesenne, S. (2014). *The economic theory of professional team sports*. Edward Elgar.

Keynes, J. M. (1937). The general theory of employment. *The Quarterly Journal of Economics, 51*(2), 209–223.

Lawson, T. (2015a). *Essays on the nature and state of modern economics*. Routledge.

Lawson, T. (2015b). *The nature and state of modern economics*. Routledge.

Lawson, T. (2016). What is this 'school' called neoclassical economics? In J. Morgan (Ed.), *What is neoclassical economics?* Routledge.

Lawson, T. (2021). Whatever happened to neoclassical economics? *Revue de Philosophie Économique, 22*(1), 39–84.

Leeds, M., Von Allmen, P., & Matheson, V. A. (2023). *Sports economics* (7th ed.). Routledge.

Palsson-Syll, L. (2016). Deductivism: The fundamental flaw of mainstream economics. *Real-World Economics Review, 74*, 112–133.

Rabin, M. (2013). Incorporating limited rationality in economics. *Journal of Economic Literature, 51*(2), 528–543.

Sandy, R., Sloane, P., & Rosentraub, M. (2006). *The economics of sport—An international perspective*. Palgrave Macmillan.

Von Neumann, J., & Morgenstern, O. (1944). *Theory of games and economic behavior*. Princeton University Press.

Wann, D. L. (2006). Examining the potential causal relationship between sport team identification and psychological wellbeing. *Journal of Sport Behavior, 29*(1), 79–95.

Index

© The Author(s), under exclusive license to Springer Nature
Switzerland AG 2024
J. Embery, *Attendance Demand in Sports Economics*, Palgrave Pivots
in Sports Economics,
https://doi.org/10.1007/978-3-031-60040-1

GPSR Compliance

The European Union's (EU) General Product Safety Regulation (GPSR) is a set of rules that requires consumer products to be safe and our obligations to ensure this.

If you have any concerns about our products, you can contact us on ProductSafety@springernature.com

In case Publisher is established outside the EU, the EU authorized representative is:

Springer Nature Customer Service Center GmbH
Europaplatz 3
69115 Heidelberg, Germany

The manufacturer's authorised representative in the EU is Springer
Nature Customer Service Centre GmbH, Europaplatz 3, 69115 Heidelberg,
Germany. If you have any concerns regarding our products, please
contact ProductSafety@springernature.com

Printed and bound by CPI Group (UK) Ltd, Croydon, CR0 4YY
27/04/2026
02097604-0003